Put Your *Money* Where Your *Soul* Is

Put Your *Money* Where Your *Soul* Is

A Simple Guide to Spending Your Money, Time and Life Purposefully

By Wade Galt

Possibility Infinity Publishing

Published and distributed by:

Possibility Infinity Publishing
Naples, FL
www.posibilityinfinity.com

ISBN   978-1-934108-00-0

*To Rossana, my precious wife, and my favorite
reason for putting my money where my soul is.*

Thank you for living your life and this book with me.

*To Ms. Agnes Campbell, my high school
American Literature teacher.*

*Your passion for Thoreau and everything
else about you are an inspiration.*

*The two of you are correct,
"Books ARE the treasured wealth of the world."*

Table of Contents

Author's Note

We can do many things to improve our lives and the lives of those around us. One way is to share our own personal success stories, things that have worked for us. *Put Your Money Where Your Soul Is* intends to do just that. On the surface it may appear to be very similar to other books of this nature. However, as a reader, I believe this book has a unique ability to help people easily make positive and lasting changes in their lives.

I have often read books which are either too far advanced for me or require too large of a jump from my present way of thinking, feeling and being. I have felt called by the author to become very brave, very quickly in order to make a very significant change. The dramatic changes promised would not be necessary if I were already so courageous.

This book can help you take the first simple steps towards improving your life. You can make these changes without leaving your home, your job, your school or your loved ones. These basic first steps will lay the solid foundation for creating the world of your dreams while you enjoy your current situation and each step along the journey.

We can choose to be happy today regardless of our circumstances (though this may present a greater challenge for some than for others). At the same time, we can begin transforming our lives into the grandest reality of our boldest dreams.

The following story is the beginning of one person's journey towards greater fulfillment in life. The character desires a better life and has signed up for a weekend growth workshop. Throughout the weekend, this character will hear different speakers, interact with other participants, and share thoughts with the reader. It is my intention for you to see a bit of yourself in each of the participants and benefit from their wisdom and insight.

The exercises at the end of each chapter are designed to help you apply the new information and insights in your life. They also set you up for success by helping you identify and take the actions necessary for achieving real and lasting change. Without the exercises you may only receive part of the benefits of this book. It is my intention that you fully experience the benefits of this book as you journey towards creating what you most desire for yourself.

Enjoy your journey!

Introduction

As You Think, So Shall You Be

This may be the most powerful and profound statement ever made. Most of us have heard about people who have triumphed over their environment after growing up in unbelievably horrible situations such as child abuse, economic poverty, or broken homes. These people have succeeded against great odds. Often they have told people (or others have told them) with great conviction that they would overcome their circumstances.

Then there are people who *seem* to have so much going for them, but they are not very happy. They do not believe in themselves or others have told them that they do not deserve to be believed in. Tragically, they see themselves as failures (by whatever definition of success they have created). It is not really accurate to say they are "failures" (whatever that means), but they are not happy (which, for many people is a far worse fate than being labeled a "loser" by society's definitions).

As We Think, So Shall We Be

Psychology calls this the "Self-Fulfilling Prophecy." A prophecy is a prediction of something that will happen in the future. A self-fulfilling prophecy is when we believe something will come true for us, and it does because we believe it. Somehow (consciously or unconsciously, intentionally or unintentionally) our belief causes things to turn out exactly how we thought they would. This happens whether we want it to or not. Whatever we think about most (and believe most) appears in our lives.

- What prophecies have you made for yourself that have come true?
  - o Did the results of these prophecies lead to your happiness and fulfillment or not?

- What prophecies have others made for you that have come true?
    - o Did the results lead to your happiness and fulfillment or not?

- Whose prophecies have been best for you? (Which person?) Whose have been the worst?
    - o Which ones do you prefer to believe and see come true?

- Do you spend the majority of your time with people who see the best things in you and the greatest possibilities for you?
    - o If not, why?

As you notice the answers that come up for you, it may serve you to decide whose prophecies lead you to outcomes you desire. It may also serve you to decide what type of prophecies you want to spend time thinking about. Doing this will help you significantly with the following section.

There are three fundamental questions most of us ask at one time or another:

1) Who am I?
2) Why am I here? (What's my purpose?)
3) What does life have in store me? (What is my destiny?)

Our answers to these questions shape our lives and create our reality. If I have been raised to believe I am a worthless individual with no purpose and no ability to have what I want, should it be surprising to find that my life turns out this way? The same thing is true if I were told all of my life that I am a special person with unique abilities that the world needs and is willing to pay for. Chances are, I will end up with a good self-image, healthy relationships, a job where I am respected and paid well, and have a sizable bank account.

These three timeless questions are each worded in a way that may lead us to believing we have no impact on the answers. It can feel as if the answers are being handed down to us, and we have no power to include our personal preferences or desires.

If we like our answers to these questions and these answers serve us (lead to our happiness and fulfillment), then that's great. We may be served by sticking with these questions.

If we don't like the answers, we may desire to change the answers so they do serve us. But how do we change answers we've spent a lifetime learning and believing? It doesn't seem reasonable to think we can change them in a few hours by reading a book.

How about changing the questions? ***If we don't like the answers we're getting about life, maybe we need to change the questions***.

If I don't like what I believe or what I've been told about who I am, I can change the question to "*Whom do I choose to be?*"

If, like many people, I haven't figured out why I'm here on this planet, I can ask, "*What would I like to do with my life?*"

If I believe life isn't bringing me what I want, I can ask "*What do I intend to have?*"

1) Whom do I choose to be?
2) What would I like to do with my life?
3) What do I intend to have?

If we wish to positively influence our lives, it is critical to have an idea or intention of who we wish to be. If we visit these questions and answers regularly, we will be amazed at how these intentions begin to take form in our lives. Doing this works for many people in our world right now, and it can work for you.

This happens because thoughts, actions and feelings all influence one another.

o The way you think about yourself affects how you act (and vice-versa).

o The way you act affects the way you feel about yourself (and vice-versa).

o And the way you feel about yourself affects the way you think (and vice-versa).

It is one big circle, operating in all directions.

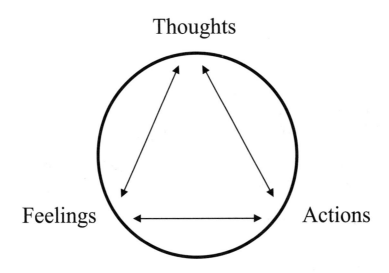

Thoughts

Feelings

Actions

You may also increase the power of your intentions by focusing on the three questions (*Whom do I choose to be? What would I like to do with my life? What do I intend to have?*) and using your answers either as goals, items to pray about, questions to meditate over, images to visualize or whatever works for you. The way you carry yourself, handle your affairs, relate to others and perform your job will all be affected deeply by how you see yourself.

As You Think, So Shall You Be

Powerful Exercise – 3 Questions

Write down your answer to each of the three questions. (We will revisit your answers after you finish reading the book and completing all the exercises to see what has changed for you).

1)   Whom do I choose to be?

2)   What would I like to do with my life?

3)   What do I intend to have?

Before the Seminar

Enough is enough! I can't continue like this. My job just doesn't excite me anymore. I know this isn't a revolutionary statement. I always believed work wasn't supposed to be fun. That's what my dad taught me. He said, "If work was fun they wouldn't pay you to do it. Nobody likes their job, unless they're a movie star or something. And that ain't real life anyway!"

Over all, I really can't complain. I make enough money to pay my bills, but I don't feel like I'm accomplishing anything. I wonder if the world would even notice if I worked or not. I want to make a difference in the world. I want to feel like the world needs my contribution. I'm not looking to make some great scientific discovery or anything.

I just want to know that when I get older, I can look back on the work I've done and say with pride, "My work mattered. I mattered."

Many people I know say they feel the same way, but they don't seem willing to do anything about it. I only hear them talk and complain. When I ask them what they're doing about it, they tell me they have to pay their bills. I don't get it. They have so many things: boats, big screen TVs, and big houses. I never dreamed *they* were having a hard time paying their bills. I thought I was the only one. I know it's not easy to change. After all, I'm in the same boat as them. *But*, I'm determined to do something about it. I'm going to a seminar this weekend. I sure hope it helps.

Money Problems

Money is not a problem until I believe it will solve my problems.
                                                          - Unknown

"Blah, blah, blah, … blah, blah, blah, CHANGE YOUR LIFE!"
The speaker finished.

The first speaker was okay, I guess. He was very enthusiastic, but he talked in such general concepts that it was hard to get anything out of it. ***I need more than just positive thinking and motivation to change my life.*** Positive thinking is good for me, but I need to learn something new to combine with the positive thoughts. Positive thinking alone stops working after a while, and I can only keep myself *motivated* for a couple of weeks at best. Motivation feels like trying to make myself do something I really don't want to do. My boss always tells me I need to "get motivated about my work." Well, *IT* doesn't motivate me. My *BILLS* are what motivate me.

I need information and inspiration. I'm motivated out of fear to pay my bills, but that doesn't last. ***When I do something I love or believe in, I feel inspired and the work comes naturally.*** I'd rather be inspired than motivated. There must be other people here who feel the same. In fact, I hear some of them talking now.

"Well, that has to be the most boring motivational speech *I've* ever heard," said the plumber. He continued, "I hope this money speech is worth my time. I could be installing a sink and making 75 dollars an hour. Right now, that seems like a better financial decision to me."

An administrative assistant agreed, "So far, all these speakers have talked about are a bunch of dreamy goals. I need something more concrete. My boss allowed me to come to this, and I promised I'd give him a write up of each speaker. He said if it's helpful and business related, then he'd pay for it. Otherwise, I'm stuck with the bill, and I don't think I can afford it. I sure hope it gets better."

"I don't really know the speakers, but if this many people are willing to invest this much money and time, it must be worth it," said a young programmer.

"You're not stressed about the cost, Miss Optimistic?" the administrative assistant snapped.

"I didn't say that," the young woman answered. "I'm paying my own way, but money's not my main concern. I work for a start up company, and I've got stock options coming out of my ears. Our stock price has tripled in the last six months."

"So you don't *have* money problems!" interrupted the 62-year-old clerk.

"I didn't say that either. I *do* have money problems! What in the world am I supposed to do with all of this?" she replied. "I couldn't possibly imagine how to spend it. I grew up in a small town, and I'm already worth more than half of the population."

"Sounds like a real problem!" the administrative assistant replied sarcastically. "I wish I had *your* problems. I've got bills like you've got stock options. Just like you, I don't know what in the world to do!"

"I'm sorry. I didn't mean to be insensitive. I guess my problems seem small compared to yours." She continued, "Sometimes I don't even know if I deserve all of the money I've made. I feel kind of guilty about making more money in one year than my Dad does in ten."

A middle-aged gentleman gently interrupted, ***It's not important how much you make. It's how much you keep.*** That's how companies make profits. They try to spend money in the most profitable way. The bottom line! That's what it's all about. I've been successful because I've helped large corporations maximize their profits. Profits drive business today. In fact, the next speaker is worth his weight in gold. I have all of his tapes and books, and I've made and saved a lot of money because of him."

"If you're so successful, why are you here?" asked the administrative assistant.

"Because I can manage multi-million-dollar corporations, but something's missing from my personal life and I can't put my finger on it. Plus, I can always afford to learn more. This talk is based on the author's latest book, which I haven't read yet."

I think he may be right, but I've tried saving before and it's painful. It's just like dieting – no fun! Every time I start saving money, I do it for a few months, but then I stop. I never seem to know what I'm saving for. I've been told it's wise to save at least three to six months of income in case of an emergency, but that's hardly inspiring. ***Fear is a powerful motivator, but apparently it's not strong enough to get me to save.*** I don't think a heavier dose of fear will get the job done. Besides, I don't want to be motivated by fear. Fear is the reason I've been in the same unsatisfying job for so long. Being scared is no fun. I want to make conscious and proactive choices about my finances and my life. I want to feel powerful and in control, not fearful and weak. Hopefully, this next speaker can help me.

Money Motivation Exercise

1) *What (if anything) motivates you to save money?*

2) *How well does it work?*

3) *How do you feel about being motivated the way you currently are?*

4) *What are the most important things you would like to save your money for?*

5) *How willing are you to try something new in order to get them?* *

* If your answer to question #5 is "not very willing," you may want to decide if it's even worth your time to read this book. (You may be better served putting your time and energy somewhere else).

If your answer to question #5 is "very willing" or something like it, then congratulations! You've taken another step towards creating what you most desire.

Money Speech

Money is a blank slate on which you can project all your psychological, emotional, and spiritual problems.

- Stephen M. Pollan & Mark Levine, Live Rich

Good morning. Allow me to start my talk with a story. Johnny is 5 years old, and he wants to buy a toy truck, which costs 10 dollars. Johnny gets one dollar a week as his allowance for keeping his room clean. Johnny figures he can have his truck in 10 weeks. He likes this idea because he can have his truck just in time for summer camp.

At the end of the first week, Johnny gets one dollar from his mother, and he places it in his pocket as he heads off to school. He's very proud of his hard work. (It's not easy to keep a 5-year old boy's room clean). That day at lunch, some people are selling chocolate cupcakes with colored sprinkles at a bake sale in the cafeteria. Johnny *LOVES* chocolate cupcakes with colored sprinkles. The cupcakes cost 50 cents each. Johnny buys one for himself and one for his best friend, Timmy. When Johnny gets home, his mother tells him he can put his dollar in a new wallet she bought for him. She says, "Just think, Johnny, in just nine more weeks you can buy your truck." Johnny realizes he must now wait 10 more weeks to get his truck. He wishes he had not bought the cupcakes.

Five weeks later, Johnny has five dollars in his wallet. He's decided he won't carry his wallet around with him because he doesn't want to make quick purchases like he did with the cupcakes. While he's watching Saturday morning cartoons, he sees an advertisement for the *New and Improved Super Duper Toy!* The commercial said *EVERYONE* is buying it, and the kids in the commercial seemed to have so much fun with each other when they were playing with the toy. Plus, one of the kids in the commercial said all the kids want to play with him since he bought a *New and Improved Super Duper Toy.* Johnny had never seen this toy before this weekend, but he wanted to be the first kid on the block to have one. It only costs *three dollars*, and he has *FIVE!* The same day, he goes to the store with his mother, picks up the *Super Duper Toy*, and brings it to the check out counter. His mother asks him, "Johnny, is this what you *really* want?" Johnny says "yes," and he buys the *Super Duper Toy*.

After ten weeks, Johnny has five dollars in his wallet. This is because he spent 1 dollar on the cupcakes, 3 dollars on the *Super Duper Toy*, and he didn't clean his room one week. When camp starts, Johnny has to wait five more weeks before he can get his truck. His *Super Duper Toy* lost its appeal very soon after Johnny bought it. He showed it to his friends, and they thought it was neat. But nothing changed. The same friends came to play with him. No new kids came to play with him because of his *Super Duper Toy*. There was nothing wrong with the toy. It worked just like they said it did on TV. But it wasn't as fun as they advertised it to be on TV. It simply wasn't what he *really* wanted. He wanted to blame his mother for letting him buy it, but she *did* ask him if it was what he *really* wanted. He sure thought so at the time. Now he decided to patiently wait for five weeks. Five weeks later, he bought his new truck.

It's a very simple story, isn't it? The solution to Johnny's problem seems so incredibly obvious, but it took him a while to figure it out. Let's examine the main points of the story.

The cupcakes represent an impulse purchase, something Johnny did not initially plan on buying but bought anyway. They did bring him satisfaction for a while, and they were something he wanted, but were they the most important thing for Johnny? No. That's the main point. There's nothing wrong with the cupcakes. They're not bad or evil. They're just not what Johnny wanted most.

Buying the *New and Improved Super Duper Toy* was Johnny's attempt to fit in. Johnny believed the commercial on TV that told him he would have more friends if he bought something. Johnny discovered that there was nothing he could buy to make him more fun or have more friends.

Johnny also realized that when he didn't work, he didn't get his allowance. He thought he was entitled to his allowance because he had always received it. He learned very quickly that his mother didn't *owe* him an allowance. He had to *work* for it.

What's the point of the story? Johnny set his goal, but he allowed other forces and influences to distract him. Because he wasn't able to delay his gratification for the cupcake and the *Super Duper Toy*, he was forced to delay his most important accomplishment (getting his truck). Again, there is nothing *wrong* with the cupcakes or the *Super Duper Toy*. They just weren't as important to Johnny as the truck. As Johnny realized, there was nobody to blame for his decisions because he chose to make them.

Like Johnny, we want to be able to manage our money rather than have it manage us. ***People who can't manage their money can't manage their mind.***

One very simple idea is to track how you spend your money and decide if it represents who you most want to be. For example, if you spend most of your money on beer and happy hour, should it surprise you if your education hasn't improved?

Changing your life is not easy, but directing your money where you want to grow is a quick and easy step in the right direction. Looking at your spending as a pie chart can help give you additional clarity. Spending the money on something (like a six-week educational or exercise class) significantly increases your chances of following through on your goals. Once you decide what you want to do, simply **Put Your Money Where Your Soul Is**. It's a beginning step towards creating what you want.

As We Spend, So Shall We Be

Money Spending Exercise

1) *What are your cupcakes (impulse purchases)?*

- *How long did you enjoy them?*

- *What would have happened if you didn't buy your cupcakes?*

2) *What are your Super Duper Toys (expensive "toys")?*

- *How have they changed your life?*

- *Have they brought you friends, popularity and happiness?*

- *What could you have done with your money if you didn't buy your Super Duper Toys?*

3) *Have you gone into debt to get your cupcakes or Super Duper Toys?*

- *How do you feel about that?*

- *How much money have you paid for your Super Duper Toys when you count the credit card interest you've paid?*

4) *Who has kept you from buying your truck (The thing that you really want)?*

- *Is it you or someone else?*

- *What can you do about it?*

Your Checkbook Tells Your Story

Money doesn't give you real strength; it just keeps you comfortable while you experience your dysfunction.

- Stuart Wilde, Silent Power

Boy have I got some work to do. Everything the speaker said made sense – but it's not easy to change old habits. My spending pie doesn't look the way I want it to. He's right; when my pie doesn't reflect my values, I'm not happy with my spending patterns. I've filled in my ideal pie and I really feel if I could start moving my spending in that direction I'd feel much better about myself and my situation. I can do this without making another dollar.

It's easy to see why my education and savings haven't gone anywhere. I haven't been willing to put my money where my soul is (or where my values are). **If I start spending my money wisely in the areas I want to see expand in my life, I'll begin to see results.** Of course this won't happen overnight, but the bar graph has given me an idea of what areas I need to reduce spending and where I need to increase it. (See the following pages).

Here's How I'm Spend My Money Right Now

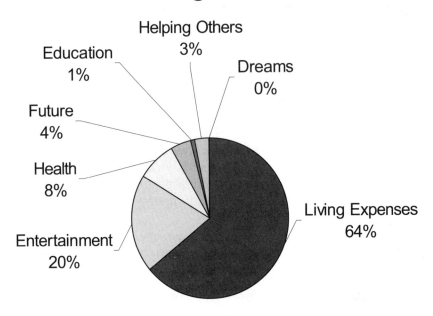

Living Expenses	64%	$ 1,600
Entertainment	20%	$ 500
Health & Recreation	8%	$ 200
Saving for the Future	4%	$ 100
Education	1%	$ 25
Helping Others	3%	$ 75
Fulfilling My Dreams	0%	$ 0
TOTAL	100%	$ 2,500

Here's How I Would Like to Spend My Money Every Month

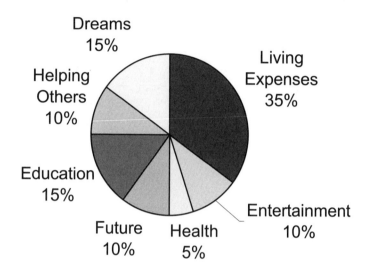

Living Expenses	35%	$ 875
Entertainment	10%	$ 250
Health & Recreation	5%	$ 125
Saving for the Future	10%	$ 250
Education	15%	$ 375
Helping Others	10%	$ 250
Fulfilling My Dreams	15%	$ 375
TOTAL	100%	$ 2,500

Here's What I Need to Change

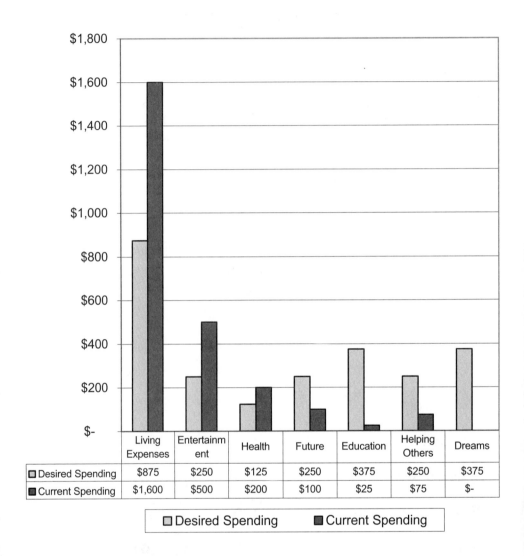

	Living Expenses	Entertainment	Health	Future	Education	Helping Others	Dreams
☐ Desired Spending	$875	$250	$125	$250	$375	$250	$375
■ Current Spending	$1,600	$500	$200	$100	$25	$75	$-

☐ Desired Spending ■ Current Spending

* The dark bars represent what I'm currently spending now, and the light bars indicate where I want to be.

I also think I may want to spend some money to learn more about what careers interest me most. I can start doing the research by myself. If I need more assistance, I can always consider getting professional career counseling. I spend about one third of my waking life at work, so it seems worth the investment. *I'm worth the investment.* I currently spend more time researching stocks than learning about my career. Based on how my stocks have done, I know I'm not a professional stockbroker. **I could probably grow more and get a better return on my money if I invest in myself. After all, none of my assets earn as much money for me as I do.** If I want to grow and make more money, investing in myself is the first step towards making more money and doing a better job at whatever I want to do for a living.

One other thing the speaker said is true: if I let other people determine my spending, I let them determine my life. After all, **spending my money is just a way of trading my energy and hard work for what I want. If I'm not in control of my money then I'm not working for myself – no matter who my boss is.**

Better spending can help improve my work life.
- *As I consciously choose how to spend my money and waste less of it, I'll need less money to live well.*
- *The less money I need to make, the more job options are available to me where I can make enough money.*
- *And when there are more options, there's a better chance of choosing a job I love.*

This is because I'll be more concerned with what's important to me. Right now it's more important for me to get a job I like than a big screen TV. Then when I can easily afford the big screen TV and it fits within my spending pie, I'll buy it (because I do still think it would be nice to have). But now I choose! My spending doesn't control me; I control it! If I can choose my spending, I can choose my life.

As I Spend, So Shall I Be

Checkbook Exercise

1) *What is your most valuable asset?*

 • *If it's not you, how can you change that?*

2) *Where would you like to spend your money?*

Category	Dollars Spent	Percent
	$	%
	$	%
	$	%
	$	%
	$	%
	$	%
	$	%
	$	%
	$	%
TOTAL	$	%

3) *Where are you spending your money? (Use your checkbook, bank statement or computer software to answer this).*

Category	Dollars Spent	Percent
	$	%
	$	%
	$	%
	$	%
	$	%
	$	%
	$	%
	$	%
	$	%
TOTAL	$	%

30-Second Decision Maker - Money

The following process will help you to decide whether or not something is a good purchase for you or not.

> ➢ Close your eyes and just breathe in and out, focusing on your breath.
>
> ➢ Bring to mind your most important money goals and priorities.
>
> ➢ Count to 3 as you breathe in, and count to 3 as you breathe out.
>
> ➢ Do this for 30 seconds (5 times in and 5 times out).
>
> ➢ Ask yourself if this purchase will lead you towards your desired way of spending or not.
>
> ➢ Listen for your answer.

If I Only Had the Time...

Why should we live with such hurry and waste of life? We are determined to be starved before we are hungry. Men say that a stitch in time saves nine, and so they take a thousand stitches today to save nine thousand tomorrow.

- Henry David Thoreau, <u>Walden</u>

Now that I have an action plan for spending my money, I need to examine how I spend my time. Lately it seems I'm not able to find enough time to do what I really want to do. In fact, it has always been that way. I can't think of a time (other than college) when I've done what I want on a regular basis. Sure, there are specific things I've done here and there, but I don't feel like I'm in charge of my time.

It's interesting because I've worked so hard and spent so much time making money just so I can afford to have time to enjoy life. Then I've wasted my money on unimportant things. **For every dollar I've wasted on something unimportant, I've wasted the time it took for me to earn that dollar.** I could spend my whole life making and wasting money and time and get nowhere. In fact, sometimes I feel that's exactly what I have done. I wonder if anyone else feels like this.

While I was waiting in line to make a phone call, I couldn't help but overhear the person in front of me.

"No, Dave, I can't go fishing this weekend," the executive spoke with bitter frustration in his voice. "Because I have to work on the Jones account. *(Pause)* I didn't finish it during work hours because I was at a stupid committee meeting. It lasted all night. I was supposed to spend that time with my wife, but the meeting came up at the last minute. I'll need the rest of this weekend to make it up to her. *(Pause)* What do you mean, 'Do I have to be on the committee?' *(Pause)* No, I don't know what would happen if I got off the committee. It's my job. I'm an executive; I'm on committees. *(Pause)* I know. I've got to do something about it. I can't continue like this."

At the same time, there was another conversation going on.

"No, son, I didn't get you the new video game, but I do have a great day planned for us on Saturday." The plumber continued, "We're going to the mini-golf course in the morning and to the movies at night. We can't afford those things *and* the video game, and I'd rather spend the time with you. I hope you understand. *(Pause)* I love you, too."

The young programmer startled me, "Did you hear the difference between those conversations?"

I was embarrassed to admit I was listening, but it was obvious. "Yes, I did," I replied.

"That executive is exactly like my dad used to be. I watched my father go through all of that, and he wasn't happy," she stated. "I guess he was just following the traditional father role. ***He believed that the best gift he could give us was to provide for us financially. He never thought that the best gift he could give us was to be happy and be with us.*** He worked himself into the ground for the family, and he never once complained about it. He simply believed it was his responsibility to do so. He always figured we would understand how much he loved us. And we did. He believed that we knew his way of showing love for us was to provide the best things for us. And we did know that. *But,* he also assumed there was a reward waiting for him. He thought once he got promoted to partner, he could start spending more time with Mom and our family. He truly did want to spend the quality time. Unfortunately, he never got the chance – with Mom, that is. She died in a car accident ten years ago."

"I'm sorry," I responded automatically.

"Thank you. But it's okay," she said calmly. "Now he's more like the plumber. He still became a partner in his firm, but he changed his priorities completely. He decided that he could either work 80 hours a week and become partner in 2 years or work 40 hours per week and make partner in 5 years. He decided to do it in 5 years and he freed up his time for his most important activities. He made sure he was always there for me, and he helped me get my first startup company going. We get together on weekends to build houses for the homeless. He's working on an English degree at night because he's always wanted to be a teacher. He spends his time doing things that are most important to him. ***That's why I don't get stressed about how I spend my time. I know what's most important to me. That's also why I don't get stressed about how I spend my money.***"

"But you have a lot of money," I stated.

"It's all relative," she replied. "Many people waste their money because they think they have so much of it. They do the same thing with their time. Then after they waste their time or money, they complain that their life is so busy and they're so poor. They actually find a way to spend their money and time so badly that they really don't end up having enough. The sad thing is they don't realize that they're doing it to themselves. Haven't you ever met people like that?"

"I guess so," I replied. "I hope you don't mind my asking, but if you're so good at managing your time and money, then why are you here at this seminar?"

"Because I still need balance in my life. I seem to have mastered money and time, but relationships are still quite a challenge for me," she said calmly.

As she said this, the lights flashed on and off, and we knew the next talk was about to begin.

Time Spending Exercise

1) *What are the ten things that you most enjoy doing?*
2) *How often do you do them?*
3) *How often would you like to do them?*

	Enjoyable Activity	How Often Do You Do It?	How Often Would You Like To Do It?
1			
2			
3			
4			
5			
6			
7			
8			
9			
10			

4) What can you do to make more time for these activities?

5) What one activity will you commit to enjoying this week according to your desired schedule?

Time Speech

I wish I had spent more time during my life at the office and doing meaningless things.

- Nobody I've Ever Met

May I ask you a question? In fact, I'd like to ask you a bunch of questions because you're the one who has the answers.

Take about 15-30 seconds to think about your answer for each one.

- If you weren't sure you would be alive in six months, how would you live your life differently?

- How would you spend your time?

- Which activities would you participate in?

- Which current activities would you stop doing?

- What would you try to accomplish?

- What un-fulfilled dreams would you try to fulfill?

Now think about this...

- Are you absolutely sure you'll be alive six months from now?

If you're not sure, then ask yourself this question:

- How would you spend your time if you had all the time and money you need?

Very few of us can even imagine an answer to such a question because we're so concerned with paying our bills. So let's start out with a simpler question.

- Does your current use of your time outside of work reflect who you are or who you most wish to be?

For now, I'm assuming you don't have the ability to change your work schedule right away, since this is true for many people. Many of us complain that there is not enough time in the day, but the real problem is we're trying to do everything. If we can let go of the need to do everything, there is hope for us. But first, we need to question our current way of thinking about what it means to successfully manage time. Here are a few thoughts to consider.

1) There are not enough hours in the day to do everything on your "To Do" list.
2) Many items on your "To Do" list were not put there by you.
3) Many items on your "To Do" list are not really important to you.
4) Only you can truly determine which items are important to you and which are not.
5) Only you can choose to not do the things that aren't important to you.
6) Only you can decide how you are going to spend your time.
7) We have the time to do anything we want, but we may not have time to do everything we want.

Think of your time outside of work as "your time", to spend any way you choose. It's important to define the word "choose" in this situation. This will allow us to see that there are very few things we "have to" do. You may "choose" to spend time taking your children to soccer practice or studying for your class, even though you can think of other more fun ways of spending your time. We all make choices that factor in how much fun some activity will be, but we also consider how rewarding or beneficial the activity will be for us. You don't "have to" work out at the gym. You may "choose" to work out because you like the way your body looks and feels after you work out. You also don't "have to" go to work or school. You "choose" to attend work because you want the money, and you "choose" to go to school because you don't want to fail your class or because you want to improve your knowledge.

Now we've established that you do, in fact, choose how you spend your time. If you still don't believe that you choose, stay with me a bit longer. You can still benefit from the rest of this discussion. The next question to ask is a big one. But before I ask it, allow me to illustrate a point. Let's say your work schedule looks something like this...

	Monday	Tuesday	Wednesday	Thursday	Friday	Saturday	Sunday
Morning	Work	Work	Work	Work	Work	Work	8
Afternoon	Work	Work	Work	Work	Work	6	9
Evening	1	2	3	4	5	7	10

...And each of the numbers represents a block of your "choice time." "Choice time" is any period of time when you are the primary decision maker of how to spend the time, and it includes activities you "need" to do in order to get a desired result.

You have 10 blocks of "choice time" to be used any way you choose. Let's say you use them like this...

	Monday	Tuesday	Wednesday	Thursday	Friday	Saturday	Sunday
Morning	Work	Work	Work	Work	Work	Work	Church
Afternoon	Work	Work	Work	Work	Work	Exercise	Relax
Evening	T.V.	Relax	Housework	School	Party	Movie	T.V.

You spent your choice time in the following way:

T.V.	2 blocks	Housework	1 block
Party	1 block	School	1 block
Exercise	1 block	Church	1 block
Relax	2 blocks	Movie	1 block

Blocks of Time Spent

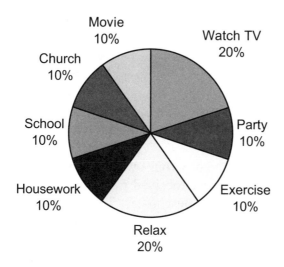

The big question is ***"Who's baking your pie?"*** In other words, are YOU making the choices about how you spend your choice time or is someone or something else making the decision for you? We all have a mission or a purpose in life. Some of us feel we know what our mission is, while some of us don't. The more we feel we know what our mission is, the more likely we'll feel strongly committed to it. The more strongly we feel committed to our mission, the more likely it is that we will act on it. However, we may not be acting out OUR life's mission. We may be acting out somebody else's.

Know this. ***We all have a mission (a purpose) whether we realize it or not. We are either living our own mission or we are living someone else's.***

We may be living out the mission of our parents, our friends, our co-workers, our religion, or our society. There's nothing wrong with any of these missions, IF they declare what you truly wish to do and whom you wish to be. Let's say you are consciously choosing to live a life of purpose modeled after a spiritual role model. This may work for you and lead to your happiness. What is most important is that the choice is (1) conscious, (2) informed, and (3) yours. One of the best ways to see if your mission meets these three tests is to ask yourself how you feel when you're living out your mission. Put simply, do you find the way you spend your time to be the most enjoyable or rewarding thing you can do with your time? If you do, then there's a good chance you're living your mission. But if you spend your time wishing you were doing something else, you're probably not.

At some point we must all choose our own mission and purpose. If we only obey a mission that we received from some other person or organization, then it is not a true choice. The mission is not truly our own. There's a good chance we will not be strongly committed to a purpose we don't completely understand. For our mission to be a choice, we must have the option of rejecting it or changing it. ***Obedience to a mission is not the same as commitment to a mission.***

Ask yourself, "Am I baking my pie?" "Am I choosing how I spend my time and my money?" Or if you are making a decision as a couple, "Am I part of the decision making process?" "Is my input contributing to the final decision of what we consider to be important?"

The same questions apply to families, businesses, religious organizations, sports teams, and so on.

Once you've committed to spend your time in the way you choose, you've taken your first step towards creating the type of life you desire. However, you've only just begun. A few other ideas are important to note.

1) *You must constantly reinforce your choices by recommitting yourself to your chosen activities on a daily basis.*

> People don't become expert piano players with one lesson. Similarly, you must continue to choose the activities that you wish in order for them to become a part of the way you live your life. It takes the average person a <u>minimum</u> of 21 days to form a daily habit, and it takes longer to form a habit of doing an activity that you perform once a week. The key to success is to keep making the same choice and act on it.

2) *Once you've determined that an activity does not contribute to who you are or wish to be, make changes.*

> This may sound like it goes against point number one, but it doesn't. The only accurate way to determine if an activity is "right" for you is to commit yourself to the activity for an extended period of time. The exact amount of time will differ by activity, but it's usually necessary to do the activity for at least three times <u>after</u> you have become bored with or disinterested in the activity. This will allow you to get past the initial high of doing a new activity to see if the activity is really worth doing. (For example, if you quit your new exercise program after two sessions, you won't get to see the positive results of the exercise program. That's not a fair test of the activity since you only got to experience the difficult part of the exercise program, without experiencing the rewards).

3) *It is much more effective to set many small goals and succeed than to set a few large goals and fail.*

It feels good when we accomplish something. We feel positive about ourselves, our achievement, and our ability to succeed again. It is often best to break down our large goals into smaller goals that can be accomplished within a day. This way at the end of the day, we can congratulate ourselves for our success and feel good about it. At the same time, we remain aware of how the seemingly "small" accomplishment that we achieved today is actually a large step towards achieving our ultimate goal. Remember, *we have to be able to congratulate and appreciate ourselves for our successes. If we're waiting for someone else to congratulate us, we could be waiting for a long time.*

If you want your life to reflect your greatest vision of yourself, only you can choose how to spend your time. Other people may help you clarify who you are, but you are the final decision maker.

As You Spend Your Time, So Shall You Be

Time Blocks Exercise

1) How are you spending your time right now?

	Monday	Tuesday	Wednesday	Thursday	Friday	Saturday	Sunday
Morning							
Afternoon							
Evening							

2) Which activities are receiving the most blocks of time?

Activity	Blocks of Time	Activity	Blocks of Time

3) How would you like to spend your time?

	Monday	Tuesday	Wednesday	Thursday	Friday	Saturday	Sunday
Morning							
Afternoon							
Evening							

4) What one block will you commit to changing this week in order to begin living your desired schedule today?

* If you can change 1 block per month, you can change your entire schedule in less than 2 years.

5) Write out your current "To Do" list and permanently remove 1 unimportant item each week without completing it. (Just let it go).

6) What do you most wish you were spending your time doing?

The Value of Time (Reactions to Time Speech)

The marketplace determines the value of your money. You determine the value of your time.

- Author

I'm beginning to see the connection between the value of my time and my money. If I spend my time doing what I like, I'll enjoy life more. (Assuming I'm still meeting my financial and other obligations. I might not be able to immediately do exactly what I want, when I want. It often takes planning, discipline and persistence to create the life I want). *But* I hadn't really grasped, until now, that **exchanging my time for something is really just the same as exchanging my money for something.** After all, I give my time to make money; then I give my money to get what I want. So money is just a middleman. I'm really giving my time for what I want.

I need to really understand what my time is worth. For example, if I make $5 per hour, it will take me 20 hours to be able to buy something worth $100. (20 hours x $5 per hour = $100). And that's if I keep taxes out of the equation. If I subtract what I pay in taxes, I may only be able to buy something worth $80 (see grids below). And if I only work 20 hours per week, I can't afford to spend all $80 on entertainment or clothes if I still want to put gas in my car. This seems like such a simple concept, but because I really haven't paid attention to what I'm making, I've just spent. In fact, I've over spent.

My Salary	Times	Hours Worked	Equals	Money Earned
$5 per hour	x	20 hours	=	$100

Money Earned	Minus	Taxes	Equals	Money I Can Spend
$100	-	$20	=	$80

At the same time, if I make $100 per hour, and I work 40 hours per week, I'll make $4,000 per week. (About $2,500 per week after taxes. See grid below). And let's say I only need $1,000 per week to support my family (about $4,000 per month after tax). It wouldn't be financially necessary for me to work overtime (even if they pay $150 per hour) if I'd rather spend my free time with my family or relaxing. It would make sense for me to work overtime if we (my family and I) decided it was more important to make the money (for whatever reason).

My Salary	Times	Hours Worked	Equals	Money Earned
$100 per hour	x	40 hours	=	$4,000

Money Earned	Minus	Taxes	Equals	Money I Can Spend
$4,000	-	$1,500	=	$2,500

The key is, if I know
> (1) What my financial goals are,
> (2) How I want to spend my time,
> (3) What's important to me, and
> (4) My decisions are based on informed choices rather than uninformed fear,

I really can't make a bad decision. I may change my mind later about my decision, but any change will also be based on informed choices. Today's decision works for today, and I'll adjust my decisions and strategy as necessary.

I'm also starting to see how this relates to my job situation. The more I'm educated as to my worth as a worker, as well as the other information above, the more I can steer my career and get a better handle on it. ***If I always have a good idea what I'm worth, the chances of being underpaid, under appreciated or underemployed almost disappear.*** Come to think of it, the same connection applies between how much I know or feel I'm worth and how others treat me. The better I feel about myself, as a person and a worker, the more likely it is that others will treat me the way I wish to be treated.

If I believe and know my time is valuable, then other people will, too. And even if other people don't see my time as valuable (something I can't directly control), I will know it is because that's something I *can* control. I will make sure I respect my time. After all, ***if I don't respect my time, and myself why should anybody else? I guess it all comes back to how I see myself and how I spend my time.*** The choice is mine.

As I Spend My Time, So Shall I Be

Time Value Exercise

1) *Who places a high value on your time?*

- *How highly (or lowly) do you value your time?*

- *Who places a low value on your time?*

2) *What is your time worth per hour (after taxes)?*

- *What can you do to increase the value of your time?*

3) *What are the three most expensive purchases that you've made in the last year?*

- *How many hours of your time did it take for you to get them?*

- *Was the trading of your time worth the purchases you made?*

- *If yes, for how long did you enjoy the purchases?*

30-Second Decision Maker - Time

The following process will help you to decide whether or not an activity is consistent with your priorities or not.

> ➤ Close your eyes and just breathe in and out, focusing on your breath.
>
> ➤ Bring to mind your most important goals and priorities.
>
> ➤ Count to 3 as you breathe in, and count to 3 as you breathe out.
>
> ➤ Do this for 30 seconds (5 times in and 5 times out).
>
> ➤ Ask yourself if this activity will lead you towards your desired way of living and happiness or not.
>
> ➤ Listen for your answer.

You Are What You Buy

More often than not, material things weigh you down – because you have to look after them and worry about them.

- Stuart Wilde, <u>Silent Power</u>

This next talk ought to be interesting, but I'm not sure I need to hear it. How do the things I own affect my life and my ability to pursue a job or career I love? I already make enough money to buy the things I want. In fact I can even afford to spend some of my money on unimportant things. I don't own anything ridiculously expensive, so I don't imagine I need to go to this next talk. Maybe I'll skip this one.

As I was walking out of the building, the executive stopped me. "Going outside for a cigarette?" he inquired.

"No, I think I'm going to skip this one," I replied somewhat arrogantly.

"Really?" he said with an amazed look on his face. "This is the one I've been waiting for. This speaker's supposed to be excellent! I sure know I could use some help managing *my* things."

"But you're rich!" I replied instinctively. I couldn't believe *he* could have a problem with things. His problem is probably that he can't figure out what to buy next.

"Oh, I get it," he answered with a coy smile. "You probably think my biggest problem is trying to figure out what to buy next."

I humbly lowered my head and tried to avoid eye contact with him. "I didn't mean to offend you," I apologized.

"Oh, I don't take any offense," he replied openly. "You don't seem to understand what I mean. I've been able to buy whatever I've wanted for years now. But it wasn't always so. At first, when I started working I could barely afford to support myself. Eating was much more important than toys or gadgets. Actually, maybe "important" isn't the right word. Eating was much more *necessary*. The toys, gadgets, and cars were still important, but I knew I'd have to wait to get them. I waited for 15 years. I worked hard and long hours. I stayed focused on my goals. And only then was I able to get what I wanted."

I interrupted him, "So you're trying to say I just have to be patient and I'll get what I really want."

"No" he replied. "You didn't let me finish. I waited 15 years and worked my butt off. Do you know what I got for all of that work? The desire to have more things. The next 10 years of my life were spent buying even more things. I was a bit of a slow learner. (I figured I had just bought the wrong things). And for that mistake all I got was 10 years older. A few years ago, I stopped buying so many things. ***I've been so unfulfilled with everything I've bought before that I just can't figure out what to buy next.***" He smiled as he said this.

"I guess I was partially correct," I kidded.

"I guess so," he laughed.

"I felt the same way until a few years ago;" a male voice behind us announced. I turned around expecting to see someone in a suit, but instead I saw the plumber.

"You used to have a lot of money, too?" I asked.

"Oh, no. I've never had much money. But I did spend much of it foolishly. And I didn't feel I was in control of my desire to have certain things," he said humbly.

"You mean *your things were owning you rather than you owning your things*, right?" the executive echoed.

"Exactly!" He continued, "Finally, a few years ago, I read a little book called <u>Simplify Your Life,</u> by Elaine St. James. It helped me change my life. She gives very *specific* ideas on how to get those things in your life that you *really* want. She also talks about getting unnecessary things out of your life. This way you make room for the things you want most."

"What do you mean?" I asked.

"How many rooms are there in the place you live?"

"Three. And a garage."

"Do you live alone or with someone else?"

"Alone."

"How many rooms were there in the last place you lived?"

"Two. And a garage."

"And before that?"

"One."

"What made you buy bigger places each time? Was there something wrong with the neighborhood?"

"No. I just needed more room."

"You appear to weigh about 190 pounds, so I'll assume you mean you needed more room for your things. Am I right?"

"Well, I guess so. But I still have more room in my house, so my things aren't really affecting me."

"Really? Didn't you come to this workshop because you want to change careers?"

"Yep."

"How long have you wanted to change careers?"

"For over three years now."

"What's stopping you?"

"I don't know. That's why I'm here."

"Want a hint? It's your things."

"Huh?"

"Tell me if this sounds familiar… You get your first job, make some money and you buy some stuff. You look forward to the day you'll get a raise, because THEN your life will be better. So you get the raise and you make more money and you buy more stuff. But you don't really feel any different from before. And you wonder how you were ever able to live on the salary that you used to. But you figure when you get this one more raise, then you can move into this better neighborhood (where the people are supposedly nicer), and then your life will be better. The raise comes, you buy the house, and you buy more stuff. Nothing changes. Again, you wonder how you ever lived on any less than you make now."

"But here comes the kicker. One day you realize you're trapped, but you don't know how or why. You're making an amount of money you had always wanted to, you have a pension plan and other great benefits (which, by now, you've come to take for granted). ***You're actually making too much money!*** You can't afford to leave your job because you can't make the same amount of money anywhere else. Not right away, at least. It would take a couple years to get back to your level of income. It's taken you many years of building skills and relationships to get where you are. You can't just replace that in a day."

BUT, the job's not stopping you from leaving. It's your stuff. ***Actually, it's not even your stuff that's holding you down. It's your NEED for your stuff.***

Your stuff is actually worth something. It's an asset. If you absolutely needed money to eat, you could sell your stuff. But you wouldn't even dare to think that. You're entitled to your stuff. You've earned your stuff. You DESERVE your stuff. And *if the world thinks you're going to leave your miserable job and give up YOUR stuff, just so you can be happier and find a more fulfilling way for you to spend one third of your waking life, well they've got another thing coming!"*

"Wow! How'd you know that?"

"I've been there and done that. Plus I affected the lives of my wife and my boy when I did. I was miserable at work, and I rarely saw my boy or my wife. But I made sure they had the best of everything. I kept holding on to my job even though I didn't like it, because I believed the best way to make my family happy was to provide for them. I didn't let go until my wife separated from me. She knew I enjoyed working with my hands, not sitting behind a desk. I had always talked of being a plumber or a carpenter, and she always encouraged me. But I wouldn't do it, and I just kept complaining about my job. It was a very unhappy situation for her and my son. Finally, she told me she was leaving me until I got my act together. It's the greatest gift she's ever given me."

"So, she got all your things now? Since the divorce?"

He laughed. "I said separation. And no, she doesn't. We sold most of the crazy things I bought. Big screen T.V., fancy cars, power speed bass boat. I decided I don't need a speedboat to catch bass. They don't move very fast, you know."

"What did you do with the money?"

"I got my financial priorities in order. I put aside some money for my boy's education, bought life insurance and disability insurance to make sure he'll be taken care of in case anything happens to me, and I used the rest of the money to start my plumbing business."

"Do you still go fishing?"

"Yep. But now I rent the boat. I've learned ***it's possible to enjoy all of the benefits of some things without owning them. And I'll always wait at least 30 days before I buy anything over $100. This way, I'll know I'm buying it because I need it, not because I have a sudden craving for stuff that I need to satisfy."***

"Sounds simple enough," I agreed. "I'll just start doing the same." I started walking out the door.

"Aren't you going to see the next speaker?" the plumber asked.

"I figure I'll buy the book," I replied. "The next speaker can't be very different from the book."

"The next speaker is supposed to have additional helpful thoughts on how to get a handle on your things." The plumber countered, "Reading books helps, but actually doing it is not easy. I'll take all the help I can get."

Humbled by his humility, I decided I could probably use the help, too. I joined him and we proceeded into the building to listen to the next speaker.

Wise Buying Exercise

1) What are the five best purchases that you've ever made?

1.   4.

2.   5.

3.

- What influenced your decision to buy them?

2) What are the five worst purchases that you've ever made?

1.   4.

2.   5.

3.

- What influenced your decision to buy them?

3) How good do you feel about most of your buying decisions?

4) Which possessions that you own actually own you?

5) How is your need for your things keeping you from doing work that you love?

- What are you willing to do about that?

6) What is one possession, that you no longer need, that you can get rid of today?

Things Speech

He who dies with the most toys… dies.

- Author

Who the heck are the Jones'? Why do I have to keep up with them? And why do they keep buying so much stuff?

Who are these jokers that keep making trendy and useless stuff we buy? Come to think of it, who are the jokers buying these things?

Actually, *we* are the people who do all of this. There's nobody "out there" doing it to us. We're doing all of this to ourselves.

If you try to sell ice to an Eskimo in January, you'll become poor very quickly. But these businesses aren't getting poor; they're making millions and billions of dollars. How do they make all this money? We're buying their products. How do they know what will sell? It's very simple. They ask us.

Businesses continue giving us what we ask for. If they don't, they die. You can see it on the internet, in the movies, the music on the radio, and everything else we either like or don't like.

The marketplace is a genie. We tell it what we want and what we're willing to pay for. Then the marketplace provides it. Businesses spend billions of dollars every year on marketing research just trying to determine what we want.

When we don't like what the marketplace is producing and selling, we need to see how we are contributing to the situation. Very few problems are one-sided. Usually, many participants contribute to the problem.

But you might say, "I didn't ask for sex and violence on television. I didn't ask for certain types of 'offensive' music or pornography.

And maybe you're right. Maybe *you* (an individual) didn't, but *WE* (a portion of the larger group) did.

We do this through our democratic market system. ***Anytime we buy something or spend money on it, we vote for it. So does the rest of the world.*** In any country where the people can choose what they buy, the people have a vote in the economic process (regardless of whether or not they have a vote in the political system). And the global economic market is gradually becoming more powerful than the government of any one political system or country. The only way to stop something from being made is for people to stop buying it. This is true for drugs, food, cigarettes, video games, pornography, and everything else.

If once again you say, "but I didn't vote for that; somebody else did. If I can go fix all the people *out there* who have it all wrong, then everything will be okay. But since I can't fix all the people out there, I can't fix the problem. Therefore, it's not my fault and I can't do anything about it".

Well, I can understand how frustrating this can all be. We all may tend to feel hopeless when we believe can't contribute to fixing the larger problems of our world. So let's see what we *CAN* do.

Although we are free to buy or not buy anything we choose, very few people are truly free. This is because so many of our "choices" are actually our attempts to satisfy our needs, wants and insecurities.

Is a newborn baby in a democratic country anymore free than one born in a communist country? I'll suggest that neither baby is freer than the other because they both depend entirely on somebody else to meet their physical needs for survival. It is only when the babies grow up and can meet their physical survival needs that the limitations placed on them by their governments become a factor.

Just the same, when any person is dependent on someone else to meet their needs, they are not truly free. So if we have emotional needs and insecurities we can't fill for ourselves, we become dependent on whatever or whoever fills our needs. This can be healthy or unhealthy for us.

> *Notice, I'm staying away from the words "good" and "bad" because we may have different beliefs about what these words mean. I will use "healthy" to mean those things that lead to our growth, happiness and fulfillment. I'm assuming, for this discussion, that all people ultimately want to be "healthy", but I am aware that even this statement may or may not be accurate for everyone. Put simply, if you're one of the people who'd like to be healthy, then this information will be helpful to you.*

Some people may help us to meet our emotional needs and wants. If this is the case, then we will be happy as long as our relationship with these people continues to work the way we want it to. If I need my friend's approval in order to feel good about myself, I'll feel good until I think he no longer likes me. Then I'll feel bad, and I'll *need* approval from somewhere else. So whether I live in a democratic country or not, I'm not truly "free." I can't just be myself, because then my emotional needs for approval from others may not be satisfied.

The same thing happens when we use physical things in an attempt to meet our emotional, psychological or spiritual needs. We become dependent on the things in order to be happy (whether they are drugs, alcohol, fast cars, food, clothes, or anything else). The problem is **things don't fulfill our emotional, psychological or spiritual needs**.

Have you ever received a gift you wanted for so long, and you thought that when you got it you'd be the happiest person on the face of the Earth? Did it keep you happy forever or just for a while?

Or how about the raise that you just *knew* would make life easier and happier and solve all of your problems? Did it? How long were you satisfied with your new salary before you wanted it to increase again?

Welcome to the mind of almost everyone – the poor, the rich, and everyone in between. Virtually all of us constantly want more. And just because you add a couple of zeroes to someone's salary, that doesn't mean it changes. If you want to know what the multi-million-dollar executive feels like when she gets her $500,000 raise, it's probably not too different from how you felt when you got your $500 raise.

If you find no amount of money or things can satisfy you, then you now know (to a certain degree) what it feels like to have an addiction.

This is where the marketplace acts as our genie and our drug dealer. It gives us exactly what we ask for. We tell it what will make us feel good (if only for today), and it responds by providing us what we want. The people who make all the things we want (the music, the things, the toys) know that we, like them, have a part of us that's never satisfied. And they know we're looking for a quick fix to make us feel better. So they give us the best "fix" they can create.

The problem is the "fix" isn't really a fix. It's actually a short-term way of avoiding the real problem. If I feel bad about my addiction (eating too much, buying too much or doing anything too much), I really have two main choices. I can work at trying to overcome my dependency, which takes A LOT of hard work and will power. Or I can give in to my addiction right now to make me feel better and tell myself I'll work on my dependency later.

I fail to realize that every time I try to satisfy my dependency by giving in to whatever I'm dependent on, my cravings actually grow rather than shrink.

Think of a person who has a big ego. He needs approval and praise to make himself feel like he's a worthwhile person. If other people compliment him and tell him he's good, his ego gets bigger. If other people criticize him or put him down, he tells himself (and them) how good he is, and his ego gets bigger. There is no solution until he realizes or comes to believe he is a worthwhile person, regardless of what anybody else thinks of him.

Care about people's approval, and you will be their prisoner.

> *- Lao Tzu, Tao te Ching*

Many of us are prisoners to the mass media and the latest trends. We allow other people to tell us we're no good unless we either act like they act or buy what they buy. Ironically, these same people become slaves to their own trends. The popular movie star or musician who sells an image to the public of what's "cool" will soon find that she has to constantly live up to those same expectations of being "cool." Otherwise, the same mass media that made her popular will be the first to put her down.

The best solution we have is to find our approval of ourselves. THIS is what we can do to change the world. We can pass this love of ourselves on to our children, too. We do this by showing them who we are. You can't effectively tell kids (or anyone else) how happy you are, but you can sure show them.

How do you establish a sense of approval? Well, there are a lot of books on the topic, but here's a good starting place. If you can understand and believe these three things, you'll be well on your way.

1) You are a worthwhile person, regardless of what other people think.
2) Nobody on this Earth is either greater than or lesser than anyone else.
3) You can rise to any challenge when you have to.

Then what *ARE* things useful for? They may help us to meet our physical needs, entertain us, help us to enjoy life in different ways, and might enhance whatever our experience of life is. If we enjoy life, we may buy things to improve our quality of life. And if we're not having fun, we'll probably find that the things we're buying aren't very fun for very long.

If you want to meet your physical needs, buy things.

If you want to meet your emotional, relational, spiritual or psychological needs, put your checkbook away.

Here are Eight Magical Questions to help you make your buying decisions. The magic isn't in the questions. It's in the answers.

1) *What do I want to get out of this purchase? (What benefits do I expect to receive?)*

2) *How much will it cost? (In money and time)*

3) *What type of need am I looking to fill? (Physical, Emotional, Spiritual, Psychological)*

4) *Is it reasonable to believe that a thing can meet this type of need?*

5) *Will this thing meet this need? (Yes, No, Maybe)*

6) *What am I giving of my time, my money and my person in order to have this thing?*

7) *Is this a fair trade of value? (My time for benefits received)*

8) *Does this purchase represent who I am or who I want to be?*

Remember… You become what you buy, so choose carefully.

If you're not sure about the purchase, then ask yourself this question…
- *What happens if I wait a month to see if I still want this thing?*

And if you can, wait a month and find out. You'll be amazed to notice how many things you don't really need. As a reward for your insight and self-control, you'll save money and create more free time because you'll need to work less to have what you really want.

As We Buy, So Shall We Be

Things and Approval Exercise

1) How have you attempted to meet your emotional, spiritual or psychological needs by purchasing things?

- *Did your purchases fulfill your needs? If so, for how long?*

2) Whose approval do you need or care about most?

- *Are you a "prisoner" to anyone's approval?*

- *If yes, then whose "prisoner" are you?*

- *How does it feel to be a prisoner to someone else's approval?*

3) How has seeking approval from others impacted your buying decisions?

4) How has seeking approval from others affected your life?

5) How do you give your self approval?

- *Do you give yourself enough approval?*

- *What is one thing you can do for yourself this week to show yourself how much you approve of, care for or love yourself?*

Reaction to Things Speech

If you realize that you have enough, you are truly rich.

- *Lao Tzu, Tao te Ching*

I've heard the phrase, "You are what you eat." Now I think it should really be, **"You are what you buy." What you buy says a lot about who you are and what's important to you.** I'm doing okay so far with the things I own; however, but I'd like to see that the things I own more accurately reflect whom I most want to be.

I can put all of the things I own into four categories, based on two simple questions:

1) Do I know why I bought the thing? (Was it a conscious purchase or not?)
2) Does it do for me what I want it to? (Useful or Useless)

	Conscious Purchase I know why I bought it, and I spent only what I needed to	**Unconscious Purchase** I don't know why I bought it or I spent more than I needed to
Useful Thing It serves me I enjoy it I value it	*Good Product for Me at a Good Price* Useful Conscious	*More Product than I Need and / or It's Too Expensive* Useful Unconscious
Useless Thing I don't use it It doesn't serve me or I serve it	*I Thought I Needed This, But I Don't Really Use It* Useless Conscious	*I Don't Need This. Why Did I Buy This?* Useless Unconscious

Of course, I want to make Conscious and Useful purchases whenever I can. I certainly plan on doing so in the future, but I do still have some things that I'm not so sure why I bought them. Here's another grid to help me decide what to do.

What Do I Do with My Things?

	Conscious Purchase I know why I bought it, and I spent only what I needed to	Unconscious Purchase I don't know why I bought it or I spent more than I needed to
Useful Thing It serves me I enjoy it I value it	*Continue to Enjoy These Things* Useful Conscious	*Enjoy Using These Things and Buy More Wisely Next Time* Useful Unconscious
Useless Thing It doesn't serve me or I serve it I don't use it	*Start Using These Things or Let Go of Them* Useless Conscious	*Give Away, Sell or Throw Away These Things* Useless Unconscious

"Letting go of things" sounds and feels much better than "getting rid of things." Usually I "get rid of" things that are completely useless, but not everything I'm letting go of is completely useless. It's just not very useful to me. In fact, there are probably many people who can benefit from using things I no longer need or want. When I look at it that way, it makes letting go of things more enjoyable than simply getting rid of them.

If I constantly let go of things I don't need any more, I'll be reminded to make conscious and productive (useful) buying decisions in the future. I'll also make room in my life to have the time and money to enjoy the things I really want.

Plus, if I know exactly why I'm buying something, there's a good chance I'm going to buy exactly what I need – nothing more, nothing less. And if I buy just what I need, I probably won't spend any more money then I need to spend. For example, when I bought my lawnmower I just needed something that would cut the grass, but I let the salesperson convince me to buy a riding lawn mower that I can drive. I didn't need that feature, AND I paid more for it. Because I wasn't clear about exactly what my needs were, I allowed the salesperson to talk me into spending more money than I wanted to. Even though the lawnmower does what I want it to, I wasted some of my money and the time it took to make that money. I want to find as much free time and money as I can, so it seems like I could have made a better purchase. It's hard sometimes to resist the glitter and temptation of certain things.

This reminds me of a book I read in high school, Henry David Thoreau's <u>Walden</u>. The author went in the woods to Walden Pond and lived there for two years. I remember my teacher emphasizing that Thoreau wanted to learn how to "live deliberately." For him, part of that meant spending as little money as possible to meet his bare necessities so he could spend his time purposefully and enjoyably. I remember finding this interesting, but I didn't see any practical application for the real world. It seemed too extreme, and I didn't think it would work for most people. *But*, I do think our society has become far too materialistic, so there must be some middle ground.

Thoreau only wore a few sets of clothing. He didn't care what people thought because believed in himself, not his clothes. There's nothing wrong with having nice clothes. **The problem arises when we care too much about what everybody else thinks.**

That's how advertisers and businesses make money. They try to make us feel like losers if we don't buy their latest product (which they promise will make us become popular and accepted). Unfortunately, they succeed (or I guess I should say we allow them to succeed. That is, we *allow* the advertisers to "make" us feel this way). Then when the "new and improved" or "latest and greatest" product comes out, these companies do it all again. So we walk around feeling horrible, and we think buying something will fix the bad feeling. The ironic thing is that many of these same business people who sell such products have the same fears and insecurities. They actually create the insecurities in each other, sell to each other to make a profit, then go right back out and buy from the person they just sold to. This is because they *need* the other person's product to try and feel good about themselves. It's all one big nasty circle, and *nobody's* having fun.

One thing I know for sure. **Now when I buy anything over 50 dollars, I'll make sure it serves my goals and me.** I guess you could say I'm going to "buy deliberately." As far as the things that no longer serve me, I'll either give them to charity (and take a tax deduction), give them to someone who would find them valuable or start making good use of them (like my exercise bike).

"You are What You Buy" Exercise

1) *What do your possessions (things) say about you?*

- *Is this what you want to say about yourself?*

2) *How consciously (on purpose) do you buy?*

- *How aware are you of the needs you're looking to fill when you make a purchase?*

- *How well do your purchases usually meet your needs?*

- *How wisely do you usually spend your money?*

3) *What types of needs (physical, emotional, relational, psychological or spiritual) do you spend most of your money on?*

4) *What are the three most important things that you currently want?*

1.   2.   3.

- *What needs do you want them to fill for you?*

- *What unimportant purchases are keeping you from being able to afford important ones?*

5) *What one unproductive/ unhealthy repeat purchase item (thing that you buy regularly) can you stop purchasing the next time you go shopping? (i.e. cigarettes, alcohol, candy, gossip magazines)*

30-Second Decision Maker - Things

The following process will help you to decide whether or not a thing is consistent with your priorities or not.

- ➢ Close your eyes and just breathe in and out, focusing on your breath.
- ➢ Bring to mind your most important goals and priorities.
- ➢ Count to 3 as you breathe in, and count to 3 as you breathe out.
- ➢ Do this for 30 seconds (5 times in and 5 times out).
- ➢ Ask yourself if this object will lead you towards your desired way of living and happiness or not.
- ➢ Listen for your answer.

Effective Relationships

If you love someone, set them free.

- Sting

"It's not what you know; it's who you know." That's what I've always been told. That's why I only got so far in my last job. I didn't know how to schmooze and brown-nose. I really don't see how schmoozing is a part of living your life the way you want. Maybe it's one of those necessary evils.

As I walked in the halls, I saw the two women I met earlier (the 62-year old administrative assistant and the 28-year-old computer programmer). But instead of bickering like last time, they seemed to be getting along.

I interrupted them as they spoke, "So are you two here to learn about how to handle office politics and relationships?" I smiled as I thought my little joke was funny.

The elder of the two responded, "This isn't about politics, it's about relationships. ***Effective relationships are based on acceptance, genuine concern and mutual respect. Politics is where you just tolerate the other person so you can get something from them.***"

"Well, I guess that leaves out office politics then," I replied.

"Which is just like romance," the young programmer said as if she was echoing my statement.

"Now I'm confused," I said. "How is office politics like romance?"

She answered my request impatiently, as if I was a clueless child, "Somebody tells you what *you* want to hear so *they* can get what they want. It, like office politics, happens all the time. Simple enough?"

"Easy now sweetheart," the elder woman said softly as she patted the young woman on the shoulder. "Not *all* relationships are like that. There are plenty of good people out there. *But* there are some horrible relationships out there, too."

"What's the difference?" the programmer asked. "And how would you know? I thought you were widowed."

"I'm widowed, but it doesn't mean I've stopped relating with people." She continued, "The difference between good and bad relationships is *HUGE*. **Just because a couple (or anyone else) has a bad relationship, it doesn't mean that one of the people has to be bad or wrong.** This society gets too concerned with "right" and "wrong." When a relationship doesn't work, both people try to determine who was wrong. 'Surely it can't be me,' each one thinks. The other person must be *wrong*. They must be *bad*. Because if *they* aren't, then *I* must be bad and wrong. And I don't want to be bad and wrong. *Maybe*, nobody's wrong. Maybe the *RELATIONSHIP* was unproductive, unhealthy or even "bad" if you must label it. But at least if you don't label the person, you don't have to go on disliking or hating them. Then you can look them in the eye with a smile when you see them again. AND you won't have to feel angry and waste all of your time worrying about who was wrong and who was right. Someday you're going to understand you're too old to worry about garbage like that. If you're smart, you'll learn now."

"So how come all of my romantic relationships play out just like my business relationships?" the young woman begged to know.

"Maybe because you're treating them the same way," she answered plainly. "So many people think relationships work like the business world does. You might think if you put enough time in, then you should get what you want. After all, you tell yourself, 'I've worked for it. I deserve it.' So you look for the best business deal (the best catch), do some research (find out what he or she likes), you develop your product (present your best image of yourself), market your product (try to show the other how *YOU* can fill *THEIR* needs), and then negotiate a deal (where you try to get the best terms for yourself from them). You act as if you're looking to fill their needs, but you're really *only* looking to fill your own."

"What's wrong with that?" she asked impatiently.

"There's nothing *wrong* with it, it just doesn't work. As soon as the deal is signed, the two partners stop concerning themselves with the other's needs. They may not do this completely or intentionally, but they do it enough to throw the relationship for a spin. Often, neither person is willing to change their schedule to make time for the other person. This is the same person they told everyone (and themselves) they couldn't live without." She went on, "If the relationship is important, make time for it. Allow it to grow at its own pace, not at yours. ***You can't schedule relationship growth like you schedule a business project.*** Just focus on making time for it and creating an environment where it can grow."

"But I do the same thing at work. We create an environment that fosters creativity and growth. It works!" she exclaimed.

"Absolutely!" the elder woman agreed. "*BUT*, you put strict deadlines on projects. If the work isn't done in time there are consequences. Money is lost; people get fired. You can't reasonably expect *personal or romantic* relationships to run on the same schedule as a *business* project. That's not to say you will want or choose to stay in a relationship with a man who won't marry you after you've been dating for a long time (if marriage is what you want). But ***the more you expect the relationship to perform for you, the greater the chances are that you'll be disappointed. It's often the expectations we have that set us up for unhappiness.*** Instead of worrying about where the relationship will be in a year, begin by enjoying the gift your partner just brought you, the compliment he just paid you, or the way she treats you.

And make sure you spend the time with the people who are important to you. My husband and I did that for each other. That made it much easier for me when he died."

"It was easy?" she asked with disbelief.

"I didn't say easy. I said easier. I simply mean we valued and cherished each other while he was here. So I didn't feel like there was anything I forgot to tell him. He knew how much I loved him, and I knew the same." She continued, "*And* he was a very successful businessman, too. His relationship skills helped him at home and at work because he was honest and clear. When a problem came up, he spoke with the involved person kindly about the issue and the two of them made time to work it out. Two of his best gifts were his patience and ability to listen. In fact, that's why we related so well. He knew that ***your time is the greatest gift you can give somebody***."

"You think time is more valuable than love?" the young girl asked.

"Actually," she replied, "his gifts of time, patience and listening were outward signs of his love and concern for people. He focused only on the person he was talking to, and he was 100% fully present with them. Nothing else mattered when he spoke to you. In fact, I can remember when I really learned how considerate he was. Whenever we went out together on dates, and other guys heads were turning away from their dates every two minutes to look at other girls, Bill's eyes never moved. He didn't do that because I was so beautiful. He did it to be fully present with me and because that's who he was."

Our world is a very fast paced world, and these days people seem to have less and less time for others. ***The best way to show somebody you care about them is to make time for them. The greatest gift you can give someone is your undivided attention.***"

Relationship Judgments Exercise

1) What are some of the reasons that you enter into relationships?

- *How much do you feel comfortable and enjoy giving unconditionally in relationships?*

- *How much do you feel comfortable and enjoy receiving unconditionally in relationships?*

- *How much do you feel comfortable and enjoy trading (giving and receiving with conditions) in relationships?*

2) Which relationships have led you to label yourself or someone else as "wrong" or "bad?"

- *What, specifically, influenced you to make that evaluation or judgment?*

- *How did each participant in the relationship contribute to the relationship problems?*

- *Without agreeing with the "wrong" person and without trying to be "right," can you try to understand why the "wrong" person did what they did?*

- *How does this, if at all, change your view of the "wrong" person(s)?*

3) How have your expectations helped or harmed your relationships?

- *What can you do about that?*

Relationships Speech

If you look to others for fulfillment, you will never be truly fulfilled.
- Lao Tzu, <u>Tao te Ching</u>

You've just finished eating the best dinner you have ever eaten. It's New Year's Eve, and you don't start your New Year's resolution to eat healthy until tomorrow. You're at a fancy restaurant you've always wanted to eat at. The waiter offers you some of the most tempting, delicious and unhealthy treats you've ever seen. You know after you eat them, you will feel full and want to go to sleep. These desserts certainly don't give you energy, but they will taste incredible. Do you eat them? Do you enjoy them? Why?

Now picture a different situation. Your doctor has just told you to change your diet for the next year because of your extremely poor health. You know your doctor is right. Your body needs healthy food in order for you to survive and for you to feel good. If you eat healthy foods, you will feel great and you won't even have to worry about your health. Your work, your activities and your life will be full of energy and life. But if you eat unhealthy foods, you will have no energy at all. You will struggle to complete a 40-hour workweek, and you won't have enough energy to participate in the fun activities you usually enjoy. Will you be eating the healthy diet that the doctor recommends?

So far, these questions seem pretty simple to answer. The first situation is a short-term question. You know you'll be dieting tomorrow, so there's a good chance you'll enjoy the treats. There are no huge consequences for eating the dessert. Sure, you'll feel a little bit tired for a while, but you'll get over it tomorrow.

In the second situation, there's much more at stake. Your health, the quality of your life and your very life itself are in danger. The long-term effects on your body and health are probably more important than the short-term enjoyment of sweet foods. Your energy levels must remain high for you to enjoy your life and be healthy. Unhealthy foods that rob you of your energy may hurt you severely.

The important point to note in both of these situations is that you have the ability to choose the quality of your life based on how you nourish your body. You have been given all of the facts by your doctor and by your experience. You know the difference between how you feel after eating healthy foods and unhealthy ones. The only challenge is to resist your short-term need to taste a sweet food. If you can do that, you'll be just fine. Your energy levels and life will be just great.

What does all of this have to do with relationships?

Food nourishes our bodies. Relationships nourish our soul.

It has been said that a person who eats poorly focuses on how he or she will feel *while* he or she eats the food, but a person who eats well focuses on how he or she will feel *after* he or she eats the food. The same may be said of how people approach relationships. One of the main differences between food and relationships (and there are many) is that food is rarely romanticized, while relationships are.

Most people will not argue over the basic principles of what makes up a healthy diet. Sure, diets may differ based on what you're trying to accomplish (for example a figure skater and a wrestler will probably eat differently), but the overall principles remain the same. We all need certain nutrients from the food we eat, and we generally know this. When we choose not to eat healthy food, we're not very surprised if we gain a little bit of weight or if we don't feel so energetic. If we really want to feel healthy, we know what to eat.

Relationships, however, are much more complicated. It is not so clear what makes a healthy relationship. This is because we are very influenced emotionally in relationships. (In fact, a person with an eating problem is more likely to have the emotional reactions towards food that many people have towards other people. For such a person, eating healthy foods is not as simple as the example above. Rather, this discussion about relationships will be more accurate).

Meeting the needs of the soul (through relationships) is much more complicated than meeting the needs of the body (through food) for one simple reason. ***We can survive without relationships; we cannot survive without food.***

It may be more accurate to say… ***Food SUADINS our bodies. Relationships nourish our soul.***

The problems in relationships surface most when we incorrectly believe we cannot survive without relationships. Or more specifically, we think we cannot survive without a particular relationship. When we eat food, it is easier to see which foods give us energy and life and see which ones take them away from us. If I feel tired and get an upset stomach 30 minutes after I eat a greasy hamburger and French fries, it is rather simple to make the connection. The only choice next time is whether or not I choose to feel tired and upset my stomach. ***True choice can only occur when a person fully understands the consequences of his or her actions.*** In the example of the hamburger and fries, I have the power to make a true (informed) choice because I'm aware of the consequences. I can then choose to stop eating this particular food. Compare this with many smokers who feel they can't stop smoking. They admit they don't smoke to improve their health; rather they have an addictive *relationship* with cigarettes.

If I can notice the same connection between the relationships I'm involved in and the way I feel, I've taken the first big step towards creating healthy relationships in my life.

A few simple outcomes may result from relating with a person or consuming food. Either you feel the same as you did before, better or worse. With foods, it's simple to choose because there's only one person involved. We can easily choose to eat what makes us feel good if we wish. But when we add another person to the equation (as in a relationship), more possibilities exist.

After interacting with someone, each of us may either feel the same as we did before, better or worse. If we both share the same emotional reaction, then chances are the relationship will be simple. If we both feel unchanged after interacting, we might find the relationship boring and not bother to spend time together again. If we both feel better and more energized from the interaction, we'll probably continue the relationship. And if we both feel worse after relating with each other, we'll probably go our separate ways. In any of these situations, the outcome is pretty simple and usually healthy because both people experience the relationship the same way.

But what happens when the two people in the relationship have different reactions? If one person feels good after the interaction (gets feelings of energy, fulfillment and love from it), that person may not be concerned or aware of whether or not the other person is benefiting. In this case, it is very easy for one person to "take advantage" of the other's time, energy and person. The person who isn't getting their needs met in a healthy way may stay in the relationship because his or her need for attention or approval is so great that he or she will tolerate the unbalanced relationship. Unfortunately, the person whose needs aren't getting met may be the only person who can fix the situation. This is because the other person in the relationship may either not know or not care.

So, it becomes critical to realize that while relationships may enhance the quality of our emotional health, we must be able to meet our emotional needs for survival on our own. This is because *in the purest sense, it is not possible to truly love someone we depend on for our survival. When dependence is absolute, the person who is completely dependent on the other is not in a position to question or challenge the other person because the dependent person's survival is at stake. The dependent person has no choice. Love, on the other hand, is a choice.*

This does not mean complete independence from others is the answer, for ultimately we rely on one another for some things.

Interdependence appears to be the most healthy and effective alternative. This is a state where we can meet our basic needs with the help of others, but we don't rely on any one particular person or group to provide for us. Put simply, the other person needs our help in a similar way that we need theirs.

There is an equal or comparable exchange of energy (effort, time, value, or love) between two people in a healthy relationship. The energy exchange gives life to both. It is truly win-win. Anything less is an unbalanced relationship.

This doesn't mean we must immediately run from every relationship that isn't exactly 50-50 and completely mutually beneficial. But it does mean we can improve the quality of our relationships by being aware of this. As our awareness increases, we can take the necessary steps to building balanced relationships. Then we can identify situations where our needs aren't being met and increase our chances of recognizing situations where the other's needs aren't being met. It's very easy to point fingers at all the people "out there" who are "taking advantage of me" (or creating a less than healthy relationship environment), but it's important to remember that there are probably people who feel I'm doing the same thing to them. And they may be right. Plus, the person who is on the less rewarding end of a relationship is often unable to assert him or herself and claim his or her right to an equal relationship. *If we are looking to create fairness in a relationship, we must be willing to examine where we are contributing to relationship fairness and unfairness.*

To do this, we can ask two simple questions...

1) How well are my needs being met in this relationship?
2) How well are the other's needs being met in this relationship?

The word "needs" is being used to represent all of a person's needs, wishes, desires, hopes and so on.

A simple chart of this concept looks something like this…

Relationship Balance Grid

	*My Needs **ARE** Being Met*	*My Needs are **NOT** Being Met*
The Other's Needs are Being Met	Continue Growth & Appreciation *1*	Clarify & Communicate My Needs *2*
The Other's Needs are **NOT** Being Met	Clarify & Offer My Gifts *3*	Redefine Relationship or Retreat *4*

Relationship Questions to Ask Myself

	My Needs **ARE** Being Met	My Needs are **NOT** Being Met
The Other's Needs are Being Met	How can I show my appreciation to the other? 1	What are my needs? Can they be met here? 2
The Other's Needs are NOT Being Met	How can I empower the other to help him or herself? 3	What can I learn from this relationship? 4

The key is to focus on what *I* can change. It is not very effective to focus my energy on things that are wrong with the other person. Many people have spent years, decades, and even lifetimes trying to change another person. The easiest, most effective, and lasting path to change is to work on myself.

In square #1, everything seems to be going well. My needs and the other's needs are being met. On the surface it may seem best to leave well alone. But it's critical to understand that good things don't just happen. When a relationship begins it requires effort, love, respect, and many other things in order for it to grow. These same things are necessary for the relationship to keep going in a healthy direction. A healthy relationship also takes gratitude and appreciation. Taking a relationship for granted is the quickest way to ruin it. If you really enjoy where the relationship is, continue to let the other person know and let your actions show it.

In square #2, the other person's needs are getting met, but my needs are <u>not</u>. Two questions to ask myself are (1) Why aren't my needs currently getting met? and (2) Can they be met in this relationship? ***It is often good to clarify just exactly what my needs are. If I don't know what my needs are, that may be the reason why they're not getting met.*** Or if I know them but haven't communicated them to the other, that other person may be limited in their ability to help me meet my needs. (For example, if I'm really looking for a romantic relationship from someone who thinks I just want to be his or her friend, it will be difficult for the other person to respond to me in the way I desire). Once I get clear about my needs, I can communicate them to the other and see if the relationship has a future and if it's possible for the relationship to help meet my needs.

Square #3 is tricky because we can't read the other person's mind. We know *our* needs are being met, but we're not sure about the other person. It's not necessary to read minds in order to be effective. We can simply start by asking ourselves, "What does the other person want or need?" And "If I were the other person in this relationship, how might I feel?" Sometimes the answers to these questions are obvious. It's often difficult to admit we're in a relationship that's meeting only our needs because we may feel an obligation to end the relationship for the sake of the other person. This may not be necessary. Usually, the most honest and straightforward thing to do is to ask the other person how he or she feels. This allows him or her to do what we did in square #2 – that is, clarify and communicate their relationship needs. Once we know their needs, we're in a better position to decide if we think we can or can't help them meet their needs (or if we even want to). This may also help to identify any unrealistic needs that may be present.

Finally, square #4 is often an easy one. These relationships begin and end quickly. But it's helpful if we don't let them out of our minds so quickly. These relationships are often our greatest teachers. A question to consider is "Why is it that two people came together and neither could meet a need of the other?" Perhaps it's just that there are other more satisfying relationships available. But it may also be that the two people just couldn't get along. People who seem to get us angry or try to take advantage of us often show us our less desirable personality traits. It is very helpful to examine what personality trait in the other person disturbed us so much. It is a basic principle of psychology that ***the things we dislike most about others are often what we dislike most about ourselves.*** Opening yourself to this opportunity for self-exploration leads to many possibilities for growth.

After all, how many movies have been made about people who "can't stand each other" and end up falling in love? Why is it that we say, "opposites attract?" Perhaps it's because these people (unlike the sometimes boring people who admire everything we do) often challenge us to be the best we can be. This is not a suggestion to find the person you like least and try to form a relationship with them; rather, it's an invitation to examine what unproductive relationship patterns exist in your life.

One last thought. All of this will work in your personal life and your professional life. In truth, there's a great deal of similarity and overlapping of the two. Some even say the two can't be separated. What do you think?

As You Think, So Shall You Be

"Meeting Your Needs" Exercise

1) *Who do you love more than you need?*

- *Who do you need more than you love?*

2) *How do you contribute to fairness and unfairness in relationships?*

3) *What are your relationship needs?*

- *How often do you communicate your needs to others?*

- *How do you communicate your needs to others?*

- *How clearly do you communicate your needs to others?*

4) *What characteristics do you most dislike in others?*

- *In what ways (big or small) do you have those same characteristics? (For additional information on this topic, read The Dark Side of the Light Chasers, by Debbie Ford)*

Reaction to Relationships Speech

Caring creates communication. Where there is deep love, words are virtually unnecessary. The more words you have to use with each other, the less time you must be taking to care for each other.

- Neale Donald Walsch

I'm clearly seeing a pattern here. Choosing my relationships is very similar to choosing the things I buy. I become a combination of the people who I relate with (Birds of a feather flock together). I can see I've let many other people choose my relationships for me. I've spent my time with groups or people who really don't lead me to the growth, fulfillment or fun I'm looking for.

That doesn't mean that the people or groups I want to spend time with are *better* than the other groups, and it doesn't mean the other groups are *bad* or *wrong*. They're just not the relationships I truly desire. **When I spend my time in the relationships that are most important to me, I feel more fulfilled because I know I'm consciously deciding who I choose to be and whom I choose to be with.**

I've also realized something else. **The more time I spend in the relationships I choose, the less stressful my life becomes. I usually only get stressed when I feel like I don't have enough time to do the things I want to do or be with the people I want to be with.** When I consciously choose my relationships, more free time becomes available. I can use that time for anything I choose – more relationships, deeper relationships, more free time or whatever works for me.

This reminds me of a story I read in Stephen Covey's book, <u>First Things First</u>. He uses an example of fitting things into a plastic jar. First he places some big rocks in the jar until no more can fit. Then he asks, "Is the jar full?" Some people think it is, but it isn't. He then places some small pebbles in the jar until no more will fit. Now the jar seems full, but he is able to then place some sand in the jar until the jar appears full. Finally, he pours water in to fill up the remainder of the jar.

The point of the demonstration is to show that if we place the big rocks (our most important things, relationships, or activities) in the jar first, we can fit a lot of other things in after. These other things are the small pebbles, sand and water (which represent things which aren't most important to us). *But*, if we place the less important things in first (pebbles, sand & water), we may not have room to fit the important things in later (the big rocks). It's a great example, from a great book.

If we make a point of making time for our most important relationships – with the people that we most love, respect or want to grow with – we will maximize our relationship enjoyment and fulfillment. The same is true for business relationships and spiritual ones. The relationships that receive the most of our time, energy and love will often develop the most.

As We Relate, So Shall We Be

Relationship Focus Exercise

1) What are the most important relationships to you and how much time do you spend with them?

Important Relationship	Time Spent per Week

2) What are the least important relationships to you and how much time do you spend with them?

Unimportant Relationship	Time Spent per Week

3) How much time spent in unimportant relationships can you replace with important ones?

Unimportant (Out)	Important (In)	Time

30-Second Decision Maker - Relationships

The following process will help you to decide whether or not a particular relationship is in your best interest or not.

- ➤ Close your eyes and just breathe in and out, focusing on your breath.
- ➤ Bring to mind your most important goals, priorities and relationships.
- ➤ Count to 3 as you breathe in, and count to 3 as you breathe out.
- ➤ Do this for 30 seconds (5 times in and 5 times out).
- ➤ Ask yourself if this relationship will lead you towards creating a life filled with fulfilling relationships and personal connections or not.
- ➤ Listen for your answer.

Lessons Learned

Don't agree. Find out.

- J. Krishnamurti, <u>Total Freedom</u>

After the last speaker finished, we gathered for a small group discussion about what we learned. Each participant was asked to share the most significant and life-changing ideas he or she learned. The first person to speak was the administrative assistant.

"My name is Susan, and I'm a support person for a large corporation." She continued, "I've learned that there are many things I can do to improve my financial situation, even though I don't make a lot of money. In the past, I used to get very frustrated when I heard people say I can do anything I want with my money. That's because I was so focused on what I couldn't afford, and I didn't know where my money was going. Here are some of the most valuable ideas I learned.

- *It's not how much I make that's most important. It's how much I save or spend consciously that matters most.*

- *Fear is a powerful financial motivator, but it's not much fun and not very effective at helping me get what I want.*

- *Nobody is responsible for my financial decisions except me!*

- *Spending my money is just a way of trading my energy and hard work for what I want. If I'm not in control of my money then I'm not working for myself – no matter who my boss is.*

- *No other asset earns as much money for me as I do, so I choose to invest a lot in me.*

- *I can manage my money and my mind better than they can manage me, if I'm aware.*

- *Spending my money on something or some activity significantly increases the chances that I'll follow through on my goals. Once I decide what I want, I need to Put My Money Where My Soul Is. That's a big step towards creating what I want.*

- *I can accomplish more good for myself with* **Clarity** (about what's important to me), **Confidence** (in my ability to decide what's best for me) *and* **Commitment** (to Put My Money Where My Soul Is).

- ***As I Spend My Money, So Shall I Be***

After Susan finished, the executive took his turn. "My name is Ed, and I'm an executive for a large company. I've realized I've spent so much time focusing on the financial bottom line, that I've lost touch with my quality of life. Making money is NOT my *MAIN* reason for working. My main reason is that I want a high quality of life. Money is just a tool that helps me get what I really want. I've always said money would help me gain the freedom to do what I want. But that meant I couldn't be free until I had a large amount of money saved up. Now I see I can be free today. As I spend my money and my time in the ways I want, I'm living my freedom now. The main ideas I learned are…

- *For every dollar I've wasted on something unimportant, I've wasted the time and energy it took for me to earn that dollar.*

- *The most enjoyable and rewarding gifts I can give my loved ones (and myself) is to be happy and to spend time with them.*

- *Once I know what's most important to me, and spend accordingly, I won't get so stressed about how I spend my time or money.*

- *My company and my stockholders have been "baking my pie." I have been living their mission, not my own.*

- *I now choose to live my own mission, rather than simply obey someone else's.*

- *If I always have a good idea what I'm worth, the chances of being underpaid, under appreciated or underemployed almost disappear.*

- *If I don't respect my time and myself, nobody else will. It all comes back to how I see myself. The choice is mine.*

- ***As I Spend My Time, So Shall I Be***

After Ed finished, the plumber began sharing his ideas. "My name is Paul," he said, "and this workshop has been an affirmation for me. It confirms all of my ideas about how I've learned to manage the things in my life. I'm glad to see I'm not the only one who thinks this way. I was starting to question my relationship with my things because people around me hold different views. It can be hard to stand alone sometimes. From now on, I'm going to stay with what works for me, regardless of what anyone else thinks. Here are the ideas that got me back on track…

- *My stuff doesn't hold me down. It's my **NEED** for my stuff that restricts me and causes me stress.*

- *I can enjoy all of the benefits of many things without owning them.*

- *I will wait at least 30 days before I buy anything over $100.*

- *The marketplace is a genie. We tell it what we want (and more importantly, what we're willing to pay for). Then the marketplace provides it.*

- *When we don't like what we're getting, we need to see where we are contributing to the situation.*

- *Anytime I buy something or spend money on it, I vote for it and I keep it alive in the marketplace.*

- *Very few people are truly free. This is because so many of our "choices" are actually our unconscious attempts to satisfy our needs, wants and insecurities*

- *Things don't fulfill my emotional or spiritual needs.*

- *If I care about too much people's approval, I will be their prisoner.*

- *If I want to meet my physical needs, I can buy things. If I want to meet my emotional, spiritual or psychological needs, I need to put my checkbook away.*

Then the computer programmer spoke. "My name is Dottie," she began, "and I work for a dot.com company. I've learned so much about relationships this weekend that I don't know where to start. The main thing I learned is that business and personal relationships often have very different purposes. Business relationships are usually very focused on achieving goals and making profits. Personal relationships don't need to be so goal-oriented. In fact, I have the most fun when my personal relationships are fun, mutually supportive and caring without the need for achieving a particular goal or outcome. It's great if my work relationships *can* be all of these things, but it's very possible they won't. I also learned this...

- *Just because I have a "bad" relationship, it doesn't mean that I or the other person has to be bad or wrong.*

- *Many "good" things can be learned from a "bad" relationship.*

- *I can't schedule relationship growth like I schedule a business project.*

- *The more I expect a relationship to perform for me, the greater the chances are that I'll be disappointed.*

- *The best way to show somebody I care is to spend time with them. The greatest gift I can give someone is my undivided attention.*

- *Food sustains my body. Relationships nourish my soul.*

- *True choice can only occur when I fully understand the consequences of my actions.*

- *If I can notice the connection between the relationships I'm involved in and the way I feel, I've taken the first big step towards creating healthy relationships in my life.*

- *It is not possible to fully and truly love someone I depend on for my survival.*

- *If I'm looking to create fairness, I must be willing to examine where I am contributing to relationship fairness and unfairness.*

- *The things I dislike most about others are often what I dislike most about myself.*

- *It is often good to clarify just exactly what my needs are. If I don't know what my needs are, that may be the reason why they're not getting met.*

- *When I spend time in my most important and fulfilling relationships, I feel happier because I know I'm consciously deciding whom I choose to be and whom I choose to be with.*

Finally, it was my turn to share what I had learned over the weekend. After hearing each of the other participants, it was beginning to come together for me. "I'm just now realizing how much energy I waste when I participate in relationships that are aren't important to me. The same thing is true for my money and time. The quality of my life will improve every time I make a choice that confirms what's important to me. And ***it's much easier for me to improve the quality of my life than the quantity of it.*** After all, there are still only 24 hours in a day. I wish I could tie all of the other ideas together better," I said, "but I'm not sure exactly how."

"Don't worry," the group leader replied, "there is still one last speaker who will help you tie it all together. This weekend seminar is the first of a series that will help you move towards greater life enjoyment, effectiveness and fulfillment."

"You mean there's more?" I exclaimed. "That sounds both exciting and tiring. I'm just trying to digest what I heard today."

"That's all you need to do for now. Don't worry about tomorrow. Enjoy today. Take what you've learned and make it real in your life. Otherwise the time you've spent here was wasted." He continued, "and I know how you've come to feel about wasting your time."

Remembering and Using What You've Learned

* THIS EXERCISE IS THE MOST IMPORTANT OF ALL!

1) What are the most valuable lessons or insights that you have learned from experiencing this book?

*2) What new **thoughts** are you going to create or embrace about money, time, things and relationships?*

*3) What new **feelings** are you going to create or embrace about money, time, things and relationships?*

*4) What new **actions** are you going to take with your money, time, things and relationships?*

5) How are you going to use your currencies (money, time, intention, and effort) to create the life that you choose?

6) What 1 specific and measurable action step will you take this week to start off your new way of thinking, feeling, acting and being?

Conscious Congruent Co-Creation Speech

If one advances confidently in the direction of his dreams, and endeavors to live the life which he has imagined, he will meet with a success unexpected in common hours... as he simplifies his life, the laws of the universe will appear less complex, and solitude will not be solitude, nor poverty poverty, nor weakness weakness. If you have built castles in the air, your work need not be lost; that is where they should be. Now put the foundations under them.

- Henry David Thoreau, <u>Walden</u>

So how does all of this fit together? We've already discussed that we become what we think about most. In the same way, the areas of our lives that develop most are the areas where we place our most attention. The areas we place our time, money, and energy are very likely to grow. Money and time are simply currencies we spend. Money is a currency of material (tangible) things; time is a currency of immaterial (intangible) non-things. The way we spend each one is simply a function of where and how we choose to direct our attention and intention.

This does not mean things change overnight. Nor does it mean we can buy happiness. What it does mean is that if we direct these currencies (our time and money) towards things, relationships, and ideals that we value most, we will begin to move towards **congruence**. (Being whom we most wish and choose to be).

Congruence is a word with a very important meaning. It means a person is being true to who he or she truly is. It's the integrity of being who we most wish to be. For some people, this takes on a spiritual or religious meaning of being the person that "God has called them to be." For others, it simply means being true to who they really are, deep down in the core of their being. (This is the person you would be if you had all the time, money and love you needed).

Congruence is a conscious choice. If we don't know who we most want to be, it's not easy to consciously choose who we want to be. But we can certainly begin heading in the best direction we know how. It's not necessary to know exactly what we want to do with our lives. In fact, many people don't know. This is because we can become so caught up in paying our bills and being whom we've always been that we may never make time to think about whom we would like to be. Once we begin moving in the direction of congruence, we will be on our way towards creating our life as we choose.

The goal for most is **Conscious Congruent Co-Creation**.

Conscious – I make an aware and informed choice about who I intend to be.

Congruent – I am true to myself and to becoming the person I most wish to be.

Co-Creation – I work with the help of others (and God, the Universe or whatever I choose to call the divine force, if I believe in that) towards making a life of my (our) greatest design.

- If you direct these currencies (your time, money, and energy) towards things, relationships, and ideals you value, you will move towards congruence.

- If you direct these currencies away from the things, relationships, and ideals you value, you will move away from congruence.

- If you direct these currencies towards things, relationships, and ideals that *other people* value, you will move towards becoming the person that *other people* most want you to be.

Spending our money on things may help satisfy our physical needs, but things alone are not enough to meet our emotional and spiritual needs.

Spending our time with people may help satisfy our relationship needs, but relationships alone are not enough to meet our emotional, spiritual and psychological growth and development needs.

Spending our time, money, energy and love on the *Conscious Congruent Co-Creation* of our world will help satisfy our emotional, spiritual and psychological growth and development needs.

All of this is about self-awareness. ***The more we know ourselves, the better we can determine what is important to us, the more effective and fulfilled we will be.*** Self-awareness may be enhanced by reading books (self-help and otherwise), attending personal growth seminars, through spiritual or religious practices, meditation or quiet time and other activities.

The tools in this book are designed to help you live out *who you intend to be* in the most effective way. But they can't tell you who you are, nor should they. That's for *you* to decide. And it's not a one-time decision. (Which is why you'll probably want to use this process more than once). Every time you become effective at living out who you are and achieving your goals, various possibilities exist:

1) You may decide to keep living just as you are.
2) You may decide you have achieved your goal, and now want to do something else.
3) You may change your goals before you reach them because they no longer represent who you are or want to be.
4) You may go beyond (transcend) your wants so that you're happy with exactly what you have. And though you still want to grow, you don't define your happiness by reaching goals or getting things.

The interesting thing about option (1) is that so many of us say this is what we want. We say, "If only I could _____ I'd be happy and I wouldn't want anything else." But if you're like most of us, it doesn't work that way. The more we achieve and grow, the more we want to grow even further. This isn't a bad thing. In fact, it's what inspires us to keep growing and evolving. The only important question is, "Does the person you're being and the way you're acting work for you? Does it meet your needs and fulfill you?"

Option (2) is what happens with many of us. We want to buy something, so we work for it. We save our money for a period of time, and then we buy what we want. This works just fine if we choose to buy something or reach some goal we find valuable. Unfortunately, sometimes we buy something or achieve some goal we later discover we didn't really want in the first place. Maybe we didn't really understand our motivations for pursuing it, but we know when we have it that it isn't really what we want. This happens to almost all of us; and it's not productive to beat ourselves up over it. *Sometimes we have to attain something to realize we don't really need it or want it*. This is not a bad thing; it's simply growth. The important thing is to continue learning what inspires and what is important to us. This way our next decision will be more effective and more true to who we most wish to be.

A full cup has no room to receive anything new. A life or a schedule full of old and unproductive activities or habits does not have room for new habits or activities. *Very often, we must first let go of what we don't want in order to make room for what we do want.* Sometimes this requires a leap of faith. We cannot have the complete comfortable safety of riding the bicycle with the training wheels AND the positive feelings of growth and courage that come from riding without the wheels. Put more simply, *we cannot have complete comfortable safety and complete courageous growth at the same time*.

Option (3) happens when we start moving towards a goal (or a purchase) and we realize it isn't really what we want, so we end our pursuit before we even get it. This is what happens when we have experienced option (2) quite often but realized we didn't get what we really wanted. Soon, we get better at identifying what does and what doesn't contribute to our happiness and fulfillment. We may start moving towards a goal, but we start recognizing familiar signs that lead us to re-evaluate if we still want to pursue the goal. Sometimes we do continue to pursue the goal (option 2), sometimes we don't (option 3). Eventually, we reach a point where we're so aware of what we really want we rarely choose goals that are not consistent with who we most desire to be.

Option (4) happens when we know we can achieve whatever we choose (goals or things). We may then begin to define our life by who we are rather than what we have, who we know, or what we do for a living. In this case, we still continue to purchase things and engage in relationships, but we don't look to them to meet our emotional, psychological or spiritual needs. Our purchases and relationships consciously reflect who we most wish to be. At the same time, we are constantly open to change and new experiences, so we don't tie ourselves down with many material possessions or confining relationships.

Every stage has its rewards. The point is to enjoy each stage along the way. The better we master our financial and relationship needs and desires, the better we become at living our lives the way we desire. This is because we now *consciously choose* to be in the relationships we're in, and we *consciously choose* to own the things we own. When we do this, we take the first step towards creating the environment that allows for total freedom (in our life and in our jobs). We move from believing we have little (and thus, needing much) to realizing we have all we need (thus, we *need* nothing). And it's only when we don't *need* that we can truly *choose*. The more we can choose, the more we can determine our destiny. If we truly believe this, it will be true for us. If we truly do not believe this, that will be true for us also.

As We Think, So Shall We Be

Conscious Congruent Co-Creation Exercise

*1) What do you **REALLY** want in your life?*

- *What have you attempted in order to get it?*

- *What haven't you been willing to do?*

- *How well have you directed your energies (thoughts, feelings, behaviors) towards achieving these goals?*

- *How well have you directed your currencies (money, time, intention and effort) towards achieving these goals?*

2) What do you no longer want that you are still directing your energies or currencies towards?

3) What would you do to achieve your goals if you had no fear of failing or negative consequences?

- *What can you do <u>this week</u> to either help get past your fears or ignore them? (One suggestion is to read <u>Feel the Fear and Do it Anyway</u>, by Susan Jeffers)*

Powerful Exercise Revisited – 3 Questions

Write down your answer to each of the three questions. (Please do this without referring to your answers from the first time you completed this exercise).

  1)   Whom do I choose to be?

  2)   What would I like to do with my life?

  3)   What do I intend to have?

How have your answers changed from when you first picked up this book?

What does this say about your experience of reading this book and completing the exercises in it?

How do your results reflect the time, energy and effort you put into this book?

What do you need to do to make the most of what you've gained from experiencing this book?

Will you do that?

People Putting Their Money Where Their Souls Are

In the following chapters are examples of people putting these principles to use. The examples are not designed to make anyone feel wrong or bad or stupid. They are simply additional tools to hopefully help you see what a huge difference a few simple decisions can make.

Enjoy...

Heels or Wheels

Heather and Wendy love shoes. They have loved shoes ever since they were 5 years old playing with their dolls together. Now that they are in high school, they love them even more. Shoes help them feel sharp and attractive, and they enjoy the process of window shopping for shoes, learning about shoes, getting excited about shoes, and everything else involved in the process.

When they were 15 they both got a job at a shoe store in the mall so they could get discounts on the shoes they bought. The shoes they liked cost as much as $400 per pair, but they got a 25% discount, which brought the price down to $300. They enjoyed working in the mall and meeting people, and they could afford to buy the shoes they liked.

After 6 months of working, they had each spent their entire paychecks on shoes (12 pairs each). Heather loved the shoes and couldn't wait to buy more. Wendy loved the shoes too, but even more than shoes, she wanted to buy a car. Heather thought cars were way too expensive because Heather only wanted the best and most expensive car, while Wendy was happy to get a less expensive car.

When Heather did the math, she learned more. During her first 6 months working, Wendy spent $3,600 on shoes. She could do the same over the next 6 months or she could do something different.

INCOME FOR THE NEXT 6 MONTHS
- Wendy's Income   (After Tax) $3,600

CAR EXPENSES
- Car Down Payment   - $3,000

MONEY AVAILABLE FOR SHOES
- Shoes (2 pairs, not 12)   - $600

If she saved $3,000 over the next 12 months, she could make a down payment on a car, and make the monthly insurance, gas, and car payments with the money she earned every month. She could still afford to buy a pair of shoes every 3 months.

MONTHLY INCOME WHEN WENDY TURNS 16
- Wendy's Monthly Income   (After Tax) $600

MONTHLY CAR EXPENSES
- Monthly Car Loan Payment   - $250
- Monthly Car Insurance Payment   - $100
- Monthly Gas Expenses   - $150

         TOTAL   - $500

MONEY AVAILABLE FOR SHOES
- Monthly Amount Left Over $100
- Every 3 months, buy 1 pair of shoes.

When Wendy turned 16, she started driving her own car, while Heather continued buying more shoes. Wendy had gotten used to buying shoes less often because it was more important for her to have a car. She figured it was more fun for her to have a way to get to parties than just have shoes to wear to the parties.

Wendy could have gotten a job at the car dealership and saved even more money of the cost of her car, but she preferred working in the mall and meeting new people. She really didn't need to have all the latest or best gadgets in her car, so she bought a simple car.

Heather would joke with Wendy and make fun of Wendy because Wendy's car was not as nice as Wendy's shoes.

Wendy would respond that Heather's shoes did not get as great mileage as Wendy's car.

SUMMARY
Heather and Wendy both valued fashion and fun, but Heather seemed to find it extremely important to always have the latest shoes on her feet. She felt insecure if she didn't have the best available.

Wendy liked the shoes, but when she found something more important to her (the car) she changed her plans quickly.

Heather understood the math, but she would not "settle" for a car that cost what Wendy's car cost. Heather needed to have the best car to go with her best shoes. Unfortunately, Heather's dream car cost 6 times what Wendy's car cost, so Heather could not afford her car.

Heather would sometimes miss parties or get togethers because, although she had great shoes, she had no car to get there.

Giving The Best To Our Baby

Amy & Alan want to provide the best for their baby. More than anything, they would most like to have Amy stay at home with the baby, but they believe can't afford that. So they decide that the next best thing is to give the baby the best child care available.

Amy makes $30,000 per year ($2,500 per month or about $2,000 per month after taxes). Here's what their finances look like...

INCOME
- Amy's Income (After Tax) $2,000

EXPENSE
- Day Care   - $600
- After Care   - $400

MONEY SAVED
- Apparent Savings $1,000

Based on this, they feel like they are making the best decision for their family. But lets look at some of the other expenses...

ADDITIONAL (UNSEEN) EXPENSES FOR AMY
- Gas to Work & Daycare   - $200
- Eating Lunch Out   - $200
- Home Cleaning Services   - $200
- New Clothes for Baby   - $200
- New Toys for Baby   - $200

        TOTAL   - $1,000

ACTUAL MONEY SAVED
- Actual Savings $0

After all that work, they're not saving any money, and Amy has very little time or energy to give the baby by the time she gets home.

Amy realized this when she spoke with her co-worker, Betty. Amy called her because she couldn't understand how Betty is able to stay at home with her new baby. Their husbands work at the same company (different from their wives), make about the same amount of money, and they all live in the same neighborhood.

Betty shared that she was taking care of their baby, and although it sometimes was even more work than when she had a "job", she loved being with her baby. Betty had received plenty of hand-me-down clothes and toys, so she didn't buy very many new things for the baby other than food and diapers.

Betty saved the money on gas and eating out, and got to nap during the day when the baby napped, enjoy playing with the baby, bond with the baby during feedings, and watch the baby grow up, rather than getting home at 6 pm to a baby who needed all her attention and getting to sleep at 10 pm without hardly seeing her husband, only to wake up again at 5 am and start the routine all over again.

At first, Betty did all of the house cleaning and cooking herself and saved $200 per month. But then she decided she wanted that type of support, so she sold her $40,000 car (with the $500 monthly payment) and got a $16,000 car (with a $200 monthly payment and better gas mileage).

Finally, when Betty quit her job, she did lose out on some great medical benefits, and her husband's company does not have as good of benefits as hers. Her husband dropped his coverage, and they bought a family medical insurance policy with a high deductible. They have to pay more of the small expenses themselves, but their monthly premium costs are less, and they are covered with their insurance for the large losses.

SUMMARY

Amy and Alan can have what they most want, Amy staying home with their baby, if they can make a few different choices on how they spend their money. Also, if they have a second baby, they will actually be saving money since they won't have to pay an additional $1,000 per month for day care and after care.

They may not have the latest toys for their baby or the newest outfits, but Amy and Alan have decided these things are outgrown quickly. They would rather have quality time than quality things.

They discovered what is truly important to them, and aligned their financial choices to support their highest priorities.

Put Your *Money* Where Your *Soul* Is

Giving The Best Education to Our Children

Charlie & Courtney want to provide the best education for their children. Charlie & Courtney both had to work their way through college to pay for it. They would like to help their kids have college paid for so that they may focus on getting grades rather than worrying about how to make an income.

The couple has heard that education costs keep rising, and they already work very hard to pay for private school now and college in the future. They recently went online and used a college cost calculator, and it looks like Charlie will have to make an extra $20,000 per year for the next 20 years if they want to pay for college education for their kids. Plus, they will have to slow down their contributions to their retirement accounts to do this, which will lead to them probably never being able to retire. Charlie decided to speak with his friend David about the situation since David and his wife Denise are in the exact same situation.

Charlie shared that he was thinking of going for the promotion for the next higher paying job in the office. He knows he would have to work about 20 extra hours per week (in a job he likes less than his current job) and travel about 2 times per month (which he does not like at all). He doesn't see any other way out.

David shares with Charlie what he and Denise have decided to do. Like Charlie, David enjoys his current job, and the income he makes has always been more than enough for the family and for their goals. Denise stays at home with the children 3 days a week and works 2 days a week doing work she enjoys. She does not want to go back to full time work.

David and Denise have decided that they will help their kids pay for state college and teach them (as they grow up) how to save even more if they want to go to a more expensive college. "We think college can be a far more valuable experience if the kids are contributing towards their education both financially and academically. We think they will appreciate their education more, take their classes more seriously (since they are contributing to the cost of them), and develop confidence and discipline by learning to save for and buy things they value. We will still get to save for our retirement, enjoy our current lives, enjoy more time with our families since we're not working extra, give them tutoring ourselves (rather than working to pay someone else to do it), help educate our children in a way we are comfortable with, and teach them gratitude and appreciation. While we feel a child's development is significantly influenced by how well it is given (the school), we feel it is even more influenced by how well it is received (the child). We both have many highly educated friends. Some went to expensive colleges, others went to state schools, and some didn't go to college at all. We both also have many poorly educated friends. Some went to expensive colleges, others went to state schools, and some didn't go to college at all. The same thing goes for public and private grade schools, middle schools, and high schools.

As far as the finances go, we are participating in the state's pre-paid tuition plan and saving money for other educational expenses in an investment savings account. Finally, we have life insurance to make sure that there is still money for education in case we're not around, and I have disability income insurance to pay for our expenses and their education in case I was suddenly unable to work.

TIME SAVED
- No Need to Work Extra Hours = 20 Less Hours per Week Worked

	Hours Saved	Work Days Saved	Work Weeks Saved
1 Year	1,000	125	25
20 Years	20,000	2,500	500

QUALITY TIME SAVED PER WEEK (Hours of Extra Time)
- Time to Help Kids with School Work...................5 Hours
- Time for 2 Date Nights as a Couple.....................6 Hours
- Time for Recreation on Weekends.......................4 Hours
- Time for Family Dinner During the Week..............5 Hours

SUMMARY
David & Denise's plan allows them to create a lifetime process of education for their children that involves the whole family and the schools rather than trying to delegate that responsibility over a 4-year period and expecting only the schools to help educate the kids. They have more time with their families, better enjoyment of work, less stress, more fun, and children who are taking an active role in their educational process from an early age.

Getting Trapped in an Undesirable Job

Joe and Kevin graduated from college together and prepared to enter the working world. Both of them loved and studied History and wanted to be teachers. When Joe received his first job offer to teach, he was surprised to hear that Kevin had not applied for any teaching positions. Instead he decided to enter the business world. When Joe asked him why, Kevin said he needed to make enough money to support a family and afford a good quality of living.

Joe and Kevin both started out making the same amount of money and roomed together when they got their first jobs. They split the rent 50/50 and had enough money to enjoy life.

A year later, when Kevin got his first raise (which was much bigger than Joe's), Kevin bought a new car. He told Joe, "If I'm going to do work I don't like, I'm at least going to enjoy the perks." Joe kept his same car, which only had 1 year left of payments on it.

Another year later, Kevin got another raise and moved into a more expensive apartment down the street. Joe stayed in the same apartment and found a new roommate. Joe started saving money since he had no more car payments to make. Half of the money went into savings, and he used the other half to save for a trip he and Kevin would take at the end of the year.

The following year, after they both enjoyed their trip together, Kevin got another big raise. He hated his job, but he was making really good money. Kevin was lonely living in his apartment by himself, and he started thinking it might be good to meet a nice girl. He went out and bought a new car and some new furniture for his apartment so he could show girls that he could be a good provider. Joe kept his same car, lived in the same apartment, and asked Kevin if he still wanted to go on a cruise this year. Kevin was shocked. How could Joe afford something that he could not afford? He didn't want to admit he could not afford the cruise, so he charged it to his credit card – even though he knew he would be paying 18% to finance the trip.

When they went on the cruise, Joe and Kevin met many girls. Kevin liked to impress the girls by always buying lots of drinks for everyone in sight. Joe bought drinks for himself, Kevin, and the girls he spoke with, but he didn't buy for the whole bar. By the end of the cruise, each of them had met a girl they liked.

The girl Joe met liked Joe a lot, and she too did what she loved for a living. She was a social worker, and she loved her work. She didn't make tons of money, but that didn't matter to her. They spent hours talking about how much they loved their work and their plans for the future to grow in their fields.

The girl Kevin met liked Kevin a lot, and she too did not do what she loved for a living. She made lots of money, and that was very important to her, since she didn't love her work. They spent hours talking about how they hated their jobs and longed to spend time on vacations, holidays or anything that involved avoiding work.

Both couples eventually got married. Kevin and Katie moved into a huge new house to celebrate their marriage. With their two big incomes, they could easily afford the luxury. Joe and Jane bought a smaller house in a nice neighborhood down the street from their friends. Kevin was impressed that they could even afford a house, but he had forgotten that they had kept their cars (which were already paid off) and put the money aside to save for the down payment on the house. Joe and Jane could even have afforded a bigger house, but they were saving money for their future vacations and for when they would have kids.

Two years later, each couple had their first child. Joe and Jane bought a new sport utility vehicle to celebrate, and Kevin and Katie did the same – except they bought a model that was two times the price of Joe and Jane's. When Katie got ready to go back to work after 3 months of maternity leave, Jane was still at home with her child – and so was Joe. It was summer break for Joe, and Jane wasn't going back to work. Joe spent 3 more months enjoying the baby, and then he took a job as principal of the school. It wasn't his favorite thing to do, but he figured it would be a good challenge for 5 years or so, while Jane raised their children. He would make much more money – so Jane could stay at home – and since he had always done work he loved and knew he would be doing it again in 5 years, he was fine with being principal.

Katie got frustrated being at work when her baby was at daycare and told Kevin. Kevin knew he could not afford the bills by himself, so he took a promotion for a job he didn't want in a part of the country they did not like so that Katie could stay at home. They bought a huge house in the new town and missed all their friends back home. It never occurred to them to just reduce their expenses.

It was too late for Kevin to get a high paying job in the school system because he had been out of it for so many years. He looked forward to retirement when he might someday be able to teach History, like he always wanted. He and Katie both longed for the days when they could afford to live near their friends again. They though about it often, but they never thought about it long because they were always too busy thinking about the next set of bills coming in.

SUMMARY

Kevin continued to work long hours in a job he didn't like. Secretly, he resented Katie for wanting so much from him. Katie continued to take care of the kids and longed for the days when she could live near her family again. Secretly, she resented Kevin for not being able to provide for her. She felt guilty about this because she knew he worked hard, but she always wondered why he changed. When they met, he was always fine doing work he didn't like because the money was good enough. Maybe he had just gotten tired of it. Kevin and Katie loved each other very much, but life just was never as fun as it used to be. They both dreamt of the old days and longed for some future day when things would miraculously change. That day never came, and Kevin and Katie retired 20 years later, only to find that it was too expensive to move back to their hometown because they had spent all their money trying to keep themselves happy in a place they did not want to live.

Joe and Jane visited Kevin and Katie every year, and continued to enjoy life in their hometown, just as they wished. Jane eventually went back to work – when the kids were old enough – and Joe went back to being a teacher. The principal job was a neat challenge, but Joe was a teacher at heart.

Joe and Jane felt a bit sad when they thought of Kevin and Katie. Who would have thought that just a few choices could make such a difference in life? (Doing what you love for a living… Buying new cars every 10 years rather than every 3… Only buying the really important expensive items… Living where your heart and friends are… and saving for the future).

Both couples got married and had kids. Both couple bought houses and cars. Both couples got to travel and enjoy vacations. But the journey along the way was very different, and that makes all the difference in the world.

Beginning Retirement Early

Ed and Frank had worked together at the same company since they were 20 years old. Over 25 years, they had seen each other get married, have kids, watch their families grow up, and send their kids off to college. They were both quite young to be empty nesters, but the kids were gone to school now, and they had time alone with their wives again.

The two couples started traveling together, and they really enjoyed it. Ed and Frank also went fishing and golfing a lot more often. After they got back from one great trip, Frank mentioned that he was going to spend a week with his wife visiting their daughter at college. Ed was a bit upset by this because he thought Frank was saving his vacation time for their next trip. Frank shared a very interesting idea with Ed, and invited Ed to join him.

Frank had more than enough money to pay his bills since his kids went off to college. He had saved for their college years ago, and now he didn't need all the money he was making. Frank approached his employer and asked if the could have more vacation time today in exchange for giving the company some additional years of service in the future. His employer agreed.

Ed heard of Frank's plan, but he didn't like it at all. Ed said, "I don't want to work a day longer than I have to work. When I'm retired, you're going to be a very jealous man, Frank."

The two work plans looked like this...

<u>Ed's Plan for Working</u> (Full Retirement at Age 65 – He is 45 now)

20 Years x 50 Weeks / Year = 1,000 Weeks   Retire at Age 65

<u>Frank's Plan for Working</u> (Gradual Retirement Until Age 85)

10 Years x 40 Weeks / Year = 400 Weeks   Age 45-55
10 Years x 30 Weeks / Year = 300 Weeks   Age 55-65
10 Years x 20 Weeks / Year = 200 Weeks   Age 65-75
10 Years x 10 Weeks / Year = 100 Weeks   Age 75-85

TOTAL = 1,000 Weeks

For the first 10 years (from age 45-55), Frank and his wife Frida did a lot of traveling. With 10 extra weeks of vacation, their calendar looked like this.

Vacations with Ed & Elaine............................... 2 Weeks
Visiting Kids at College and In Their New Homes...... 2 Weeks
Extra Vacation Cruise & Fishing Trip..................... 2 Weeks
Visiting Other Family & Grandkids........................ 4 Weeks
Relaxing at Home Doing Nothing.......................... 2 Weeks

Frank and Frida got to spend more time traveling, and they were much more involved in their children's lives. Frank and Frida spent 2 weeks with each of their children each year. Eventually their children had grandchildren, and they got to visit them, too. Frank was still very involved at work, but he simply was there a little less often. Ed and Elaine watched Frank and Frida enjoy their time and looked forward to the days when Ed would retire.

For the next 10 years (from age 55-65), Frank and his wife Frida did even more traveling. With 10 extra weeks of vacation, their calendar looked like this.

Vacations with Ed & Elaine............................... 2 Weeks
Visiting Kids & Grandkids .... 8 Weeks
Extra Vacation Cruise & Fishing Trips.................... 4 Weeks
Visiting Other Family .... 4 Weeks
Relaxing at Home Doing Nothing.......................... 2 Weeks
Volunteering / Building Homes in Another Country.... 2 Weeks

Frank and Frida got to watch their grandchildren grow up even though they did not live in the same town. Ed and Elaine missed this part of life. Frank and Frida also got to connect with other members of their family over the 20 years since Frank went into gradual retirement. Some of the family members that Frank and Frida visited had died over the years. This was painful, but not as painful as it would have been if they did not get to spend time with them over the years. Ed and Elaine had relatives who died, too, but all they had was regret over not having seen their relatives for years and only hearing of their deaths after they happened or shortly before, when it was too late to visit or enjoy their company.

When Ed finally retired, he and Elaine made many vacation plans. They added 10 weeks of vacation to their plans and another 20 weeks of visiting family. Frank and Frida joined them for many of their extra 10 weeks of vacation and spent some more time with their families and volunteering.

When Ed and Elaine visited their kids, their grandkids were just about to go off to college. The grandkids were happy to see their grandparents, but they were at an age where they most wanted to spend time with their friends, rather than their grandparents. Ed and Elaine's kids were busy with their own lives, too, and after a while it felt a bit awkward to be around their kids and their kids' spouses when they really didn't know them very well. After all, it had been over 20 years since their kids lived at home, and their kids each met their spouses at college. Ed and Elaine only got to know the spouses briefly on random but rare visits.

When Ed was at home, he was quite bored. He and Elaine had not spent large amounts of time together as a couple over the years, other than weekends. He was used to doing work, and she had her routines, too. Ed missed his friends as work, and after a while, he wished he were working every other week like Frank was. Ed felt very old. He was only 65 years old, but he wasn't really involved in anything. He even asked to return to work on a part-time basis, but they really didn't have room for him. Frank and the company had spent 20 years figuring out how to best have him help the company in short amounts of time. Frank learned many new skills over the years and was a highly valuable project team member. Because of the flexibility of his work schedule, Frank got involved in many different projects over the years, while Ed stayed in the same department. Ed's old department offered him to come back and work full time or to work 20 hours per week in half days (which he did not want), but they weren't very flexible otherwise.

The worst thing was that Ed wasn't as young as he used to be. He wasn't dead at 65, but there were things he could do when he was 45 and 55 that he couldn't do now. Ed and Elaine were now too old to do the adventure trips that Frank and Frida did when they were 45 and 55. Ed knew, as he got older this would only get worse.

From age 75 to 85, things continued in a similar way. Frank decided to keep working 20 weeks / year since he enjoyed his work so much, and Ed kept regretting a decision he made 40 years ago.

SUMMARY

One simple decision allowed Frank and Frida to live their lives more fully each day. One simple decision kept Ed and Elaine waiting and hoping for a tomorrow that wasn't as bright as it could have been. Many couples like Ed and Elaine find that one of them passes away before they even get to enjoy retirement together.

By enjoying today and every day, Frank and Frida made sure they didn't let life pass them by. Their lives gradually became fuller and richer and more involved with family, friends, and fun every year.

Ed and Elaine kept waiting on a dream life that would magically appear when their 65th birthdays appeared. That dream life never arrived.

Author's Last Word

I have done my best to write this book in a practical and simple manner. To avoid philosophical, religious and spiritual issues, I have made few references to my spiritual beliefs. God and the Universe play a significant role in my life and my success. I attribute many of the positive accomplishments in my life to a "higher power." In my experience, adding spirituality to this process makes it incredibly more successful. But that's MY understanding.

I believe the principles and ideas in this book are universal and practical. Put simply, they work. These ideas have touched those who do believe in a higher power and those who do not.

Any process, idea, group, or practice leading to growth, self-discovery and development will enhance the results you receive from living this book.

I hope this book becomes, for you, one of those opportunities in your life when you choose to move forward, become an active creator in your life and begin making your dreams real.

Thank you for joining me on the journey towards *Conscious Congruent Co-Creation*.

I wish you Peace, Happiness, and Fulfillment.

Sincerely,

Wade Galt

<u>Acknowledgments</u>

This book was co-created through the help of many who inspire me, support me, believe in me, challenge me, and bring out the best in me. I thank and love all of you.

God, Ms. Campbell, Rossana, Francisco, Mom, Dad, Natalie, Christian, Brad, Madison, Mason, Matthew, Wally, Sting, Thoreau, Stuart, Deepak, Neale, Stephen & Mark, Shakti, Elaine, Stephen, Debbie, Tino, Rhonda, Simon, Patrick, Pablo, Pilar, Mariana, Gonzalo, Marianita, Gonzalito, Samantha, Santiago, Susan, Joan & Greg, Sean & Beckey, Christy, Kyla, Jordan, Danielle, Stephanie, and everyone else not listed here who has helped me see the divine within me.

I am truly privileged to have such friends and supporters. I believe we reap what we sow 100 times over. I have reaped so much. I am inspired to sow even more.

About the Author

Wade has worked successfully as a personal life coach, organizational coach, computer trainer, sales consultant, executive coach, speaker, mental health counselor, management consultant, software designer and programmer, author, business analyst, financial counselor, employee recruiter, and in many other capacities.

Wade has a Bachelor's degree in Marketing and a Master's degree in Mental Health Counseling Psychology.

He lives happily with his beautiful wife, their gorgeous son and loving dog.

His email address is wade@wadegalt.com .

<u>Other Helpful Reading</u> *

<u>The Dark Side of the Light Chasers</u>, by Debbie Ford

<u>First Things First</u> by Stephen Covey

<u>Feel the Fear and Do It Anyway</u> by Susan Jeffers

<u>Die Broke</u> and <u>Live Rich</u> by Stephen M. Pollan and Mark Levine

<u>The Seven Spiritual Laws of Success</u> by Deepak Chopra

<u>Silent Power</u> by Stuart Wilde

<u>Simplify Your Life</u> by Elaine St. James

<u>The Tao te Ching, A New English Version</u> by Stephen Mitchell

<u>True Prosperity</u> by Shakti Gawain

<u>Walden</u> by Henry David Thoreau

* The author does not agree with every opinion and point of view presented in every book; however, these books have been a great source of thought provoking material for the author.

To participate in workshops to implement these insights and / or purchase other powerful books, go to <u>www.possibilityinfinity.com</u>.

Part of the profit from the sale of these books goes to organizations and charities that seek to end unnecessary hunger and poverty.

Bulk purchases of this book for educational or non-profit purposes may be made at a price slightly above cost.